3 TIPS

3 TIPS

THE ESSENTIALS FOR PEACE, JOY AND SUCCESS

MEERA GANDHI

RUPA

Published by
Rupa Publications India Pvt. Ltd 2022
7/16, Ansari Road, Daryaganj
New Delhi 110002

Sales centres:
Allahabad Bengaluru Chennai
Hyderabad Jaipur Kathmandu
Kolkata Mumbai

Text coordination: Reza Hussain

P-ISBN: 978-93-5520-878-1
E-ISBN: 978-93-5520-879-8

Third impression 2023

10 9 8 7 6 5 4 3

The moral right of the author has been asserted.

Printed in India

*"We are to the Universe only
as much as we give back to it."*

๛

CONTENTS

On Life

On Self

OPENING THOUGHTS

My dear reader,

This book is a collection of the learnings I've gleaned through my life experiences as a philanthropist, mother, businesswoman and as one fraction of the universal spirit that we are all a part of.

These tips are meant to serve as a guide that you can refer to when you find yourself in conflict—whether inner or external—or just need some quick, utterly practical advice on any of the dozens of topics, situations and scenarios covered herein.

However, I believe we already have *all* the answers we seek inside us. I believe that if we are in perfect harmony with the universe and if we practise small steps such as eating right, sleeping well and not letting stress get the better of us, we can make the best decisions for ourselves almost intuitively!

If we find ourselves hitting dead ends, we have to take some time to dig deeper, do some soul-searching and then, accept reality for what it is. But trust me, *change*, no matter how challenging or difficult, is always for the best! The probability of being born on this planet is the product of a confluence of factors that are largely left up to chance, so *each* one of us is very special. The universe, in turn, wants to take care of us.

Take time to think about what *you* truly want for yourself. Once you are clear and put your intentions out there, a path is set in motion and the outcome will be favourable. We are the initiators, and once we detach ourselves from the result, the desired outcome will be reached.

Be your most powerful, best and strongest self!

This is *your* journey, and only one person can take it—you. The world is an endless sea of gifts that appear in the form of opportunities. Receive freely and give freely to live your most authentic life and be your best self.

I wish you an abundance of peace and joy!

Meera Gandhi

WHY 3 TIPS:
A NOTE BEFORE WE BEGIN

I believe that life can be made simple and beautiful by sharing knowledge and by helping each other. This book is my attempt to share some of the wisdom I have acquired along the way through three simple tips on each subject.

Today I feel spiritually alive and connected to our planet. It is my belief that our journey on earth is one that we share with all living beings and it leads us towards one common goal: happiness.

In fact, the pursuit of happiness preoccupies our thoughts and energy. Think of the last five conscious efforts you've made. How many of them were for pleasure or contentment? From the cradle to the grave, practically every human that has walked on this earth has sought their share of this invisible bounty.

Several Worldwide Gallup polls and decades-long scientific studies have been dedicated to understanding happiness. There (in the US) many acclaimed colleges are developing courses on 'finding happiness'. Hundreds of years of poetry, art and music all around the world have been dedicated to this most basic human desire!

Books, rituals and individual achievements often bring us happiness, and so do certain activities and behavioural changes. Yet, for all the collective human effort and yearning for this wonderful condition, doesn't it seem like happiness is elusive to many?

Why is this the case? Why do so many people who have every material comfort seem so unhappy, while others, who possess practically nothing, are able to produce a totally joyful smile even in the midst of what we perceive as agony?

This book provides answers to such questions. I believe that a happier life can be lived by resolving many small, everyday problems through these tips for almost *every* situation in life. I categorize them into three major categories: work, life and self.In *3 Tips*, I attempt to give you, the reader, the tools to cultivate and sustain a joyful energy, and to live a joyful life. The book is an ecstatic exploration of the many ways through which we can truly forge our own path towards lasting happiness.

Please enjoy the thoughts. Here's to the joy that's within all of us.

ON WORK

3 TIPS ON HOW TO GET THE BEST OUT OF YOUR EDUCATION

- Write clearly: Learn to be direct and forthright while writing.

- Express yourself convincingly: Learn to make readers truly understand.

- Think analytically: Develop critical thinking skills. By thinking critically, one can weigh options sensibly and make the best decision for oneself and others in *every* situation.

Education is the gift of information that is passed down to us from other people's experiences. We get this informational input so we can use it as a springboard, utilizing this treasure trove of knowledge we don't have to labour to learn first-hand. Once I understood this, I started learning with gusto, knowing that all this knowledge was a gift that was going to make my life easier, and my choices more informed. I also hoped that it would help me find the answers to some of the existential questions posed by my soul from time to time. Throughout their childhood and even later, I encouraged my three children to love learning. School and college can be a very happy time in life, and I always communicated this to my children by being present at all school events and making their school and college life a top priority. A love for learning is key to growth and a calm, successful life!

Armed with education, we have to add our unique thinking to the mix and express our thoughts clearly—in speech and writing—and also think analytically while listening to our consciousness, the best guide. Utilizing information provided by our education, enables us to glide through life, making good decisions for ourselves and others and creating win-win outcomes for all!

Although learning is a lifelong enterprise, the thought of education takes me back to my own years at school. My family moved a lot due to my father's work, and we kept shuttling across three major cities in India—Pune, Mumbai and Delhi. I studied at St. Anne's in Pune, then the Convent of Jesus and Mary in Delhi. When we moved to Mumbai, I went to St. Anne's in Fort, Mumbai, and then The Cathedral and John Connon School for my high school years. Each of these formative school years stressed on clear writing skills, but Cathedral in Mumbai really taught me how to express myself convincingly. Debate and elocution are taken seriously at Cathedral! At the United World College, I learnt how to make decisions that had a positive impact on the entire community of students. The clear ideology of win-win was instilled in me at the United World College. Later, I went to Boston University where I got my MBA and learned more sophisticated analytical skills. My journey of learning didn't stop there as every day brings forth a teaching moment. We just have to be aware of what we are learning, from where and from whom, so that we can utilize those skills when the right time comes.

3 TIPS ON HARD WORK

- Hard work creates accomplishments: Hard work initially feels difficult, but through hard work we can accomplish much; and accomplishment itself is joy.

- We must work hard: Through hard work we learn that we are competent and able, and can handle anything.

- Hard work connects us: Know that accomplishment at an individual level is connected to accomplishment on a universal level. We are connected to the universe through our hard work. In turn, it connects us to the universal energy on earth.

'Work is love made visible,' said Kahlil Gibran, and these words have held true in my own life. When I understood that my individual effort is definitely connected to accomplishment on a universal level, it gave me faith and confidence. I was able to understand that we are not alone in our endeavours. Many other forces—visible and invisible—are supporting our efforts. Is this not a powerful piece of knowledge to keep in our minds as we give our all to the work we undertake?

The harder we work, the more competent we become, and the more knowledge we gain. This makes hard work easier and easier over time. These are gained skills we can pass on to the younger generations so they may accomplish the same tasks with greater ease. We also know that we will have newer technologies at hand, taking the planet's accomplishments to a higher degree of sophistication and complexity, while making the task easier to accomplish. This is, after all, how we evolve. This is the story of evolution!

I remember that for a time during my childhood we lived in Pune, at the Indian Institute of Armament Technology campus. My father had found a spot on the Khadakwasla Lake, and grown fond of taking a small boat out every evening. Then, he had a small jetty built. Every day after his office closed, my father would go there to oversee the construction. Many days after school, I would be on the waterfront, watching the digging and building as the marina took shape. It was soon named 'The Naval Experimental Bay' and today, an expanded version of the same stands proudly, with boats docking on it and several events being held there. It was, and is, a product of hard work and one man's vision. Thus, at the young age of seven *I learnt that if you think of something, you can certainly do it.* Hard work and perseverance are the only things we need to accomplish it all!

Accomplishment is joy and happiness, and together they are the reason why we are on this planet. Therefore, hard work that can benefit others as well as ourselves is a very important part of our journey on earth. Think of it as fun and it will be fun, think of it as easy and it will be easy, just ascertain whether it's useful or not and then proceed accordingly!

Here's to hard work and joyfulness!

3 TIPS TO ACCOMPLISH AND SUCCEED IN YOUR WORK LIFE

- Do your best: Perform any task you are doing to the very best of your ability. With determination, you will be able to accomplish any task and any goal.

- Don't hurt others: Do not accomplish things at the cost of anyone in the short or long run. Accomplishing things to the detriment of others will inhibit your ability to be truly successful in the long run.

- Believe in your work: Believe in what you are doing. Self-confidence is essential to accomplishing a goal successfully.

Success is seen as the measure of one's will. Those with the strongest will and the dedication to back it succeed. But is that all there is to it? I think there is an even simpler definition. The formula to becoming an accomplished person is simple. Perform your work to the best of your ability in every given moment. That's it! Nothing more is needed!

I remember attending a sewing class at the Convent of Jesus and Mary School in Delhi. I was six years old, and was working on the embroidery for a tea cosy. I was painstakingly sewing in the outline of the red flowers in 'chain stitch' and filling the petals in to give the flowers depth.

Before I knew it, the bell rang and my neighbour said, 'Oops! You did not finish the green stems! We were supposed to have all that done. The teacher will be so mad at you!'

I was nervous as I took my work up to the needlework teacher's desk. She looked at my embroidery and said, 'This is flawless.' She held it up to the class and said, 'Look at this example of neat work. All of you should talk less and focus on doing such beautiful work.'

'But I did not get to the green stems,' I said softly.

'Yes, I see that,' said the teacher kindly. 'You will have to come in five minutes early for the next class, missing five minutes of break time, so that you can get this done.'

She was smiling. 'But your work is excellent,' she added.

This is one of my earliest memories of being commended for my work. I understood the power of excellence and enjoyed the feeling of doing my best and knowing that it was the way forward. While working hard on our personal goals, we have to believe in them and accomplish them without hurting anyone—even ourselves—in the process. These ideas have led many great people to accomplish their ideas with ease and success.

When I think about success, I remember the cycling race organized by the Jaycee Committee in 1978. I was then a teenager in Mumbai. I loved bicycling and wanted to take part in the amateur cycling race, which was to start at the Flora restaurant in Worli and end at the Oberoi Hotel at Nariman Point. I told my parents that I wanted to participate and they said that I had to practice the route and work hard if I wanted to succeed. I wanted to accomplish more than just finishing the race; I wanted to win the race. My father said he would help me. Every morning, at 5 a.m., he would drive me and my bike to the Flora restaurant and I would get down with my bike and ride the route; my father would drive the car alongside, encouraging me. On the day of the race, I felt strong and calm. I had worked hard and was excited about the race. The race flagged off and I started cycling. I gave it my best and kept going strong. As I was biking, I could hear people cheering along the roadside. I realized they were cheering me on as I was ahead in the race. I was the leader and quite a bit ahead of the other cyclists. I kept on giving it my best shot and soon saw the finish line ribbon, and crossed it. It felt so good that I had won the race and that my hard work had paid off. I was just fifteen and I could see the joy and pride on the faces of my parents and my younger brother and sister. I went to hug and thank my father for waking up so early every day—before his long day of work—to help me practise for this race!

When the time came for the medals to be presented, I received a terrible blow. I was told that I was disqualified since I was not an 'amateur' cyclist. They said that I came in three kilometres ahead of the girl who came in second; there was no way I was an amateur! The girl who finished second was the daughter of someone in the Jaycee Committee, and it seemed like they used the 'not amateur' argument as an excuse to disqualify me. I was very disappointed, and even more so for having seen the sadness in my father's eyes. It crushed me. I did not mind my hard work being in vain, but my father had woken up each day with so much love and dedication. It was unfair and that moment hurt me more than anything in life.

When we got home, my father called me and said, 'You are a champion in my eyes. We are *so* proud of you! You won the race and were successful and no one can take that away from you!' His words have stayed with me. Isn't it worth more than any medal?

This incident taught me the meaning of success. I learnt to ascertain what success means to me and that I don't have to prove anything to anyone. The feeling of knowing that I have done my best and succeeded is the best and truest feeling of success!

3 TIPS ON TRYING TO MAKE A TRAVEL OR SCHEDULING DECISION

- Schedule correctly: When you hear the proposed date of travel, ask yourself whether it sounds comfortable or stressful.

- Be flexible: If the date of travel sounds stressful and unaligned with current happenings, reschedule!

- Prioritize: Ask yourself whether you really need this trip or not. Can the same thing be accomplished by phone or video conference? Prioritize time.

Travel has been one of the definitive factors in my life, just as it is in the lives of millions. It is how I gain a deeper understanding of the world and its many glorious cultures, languages and people. My travel experiences have always been a source of great joy and learning to me. No matter the original purpose of each trip, I always try to make the most of it by trying something new, visiting family, or meeting an old friend along the way. Adopting a multitasking mindset also helps you adopt a mindset of flexibility. By structuring your time, this rule can be applied to so many other aspects of your life.

However, like anything else, too much travel is not a good idea.

I wrote down these tips before most travel came to a grinding halt at the onset of the COVID-19 pandemic. I was starting to feel the stress of travelling constantly and it was becoming very unsettling. It's not like I had much of a choice in the matter either. My three children were studying in London, Rhode Island and Washington, DC, while I was living between Hong Kong and India, managing home and the demands of a married life, and running the Giving Back Foundation. It was a thinly spread existence! I was caught in a cycle of planning, packing, travelling, arriving, unpacking, attending meetings or meeting family, packing for the trip back, and repeating each step all over again. It was very exhausting, important as it was, and joyful as I could see and guide my children!

My takeaway from these years of extensive travel was simple: if you don't absolutely need to take the trip, try to find a solution by videoconferencing. If you are too busy, find another date to travel. Finally, when you do decide to take the trip, pack calmly, meditate on the plane and enjoy the trip. If you are going to go the mile anyway, you might as well enjoy the trip!

3 TIPS ON BEING A GOOD LEADER

- Be compassionate: Compassion is the emotional trait that enables managers to become strong leaders.

- Deliver on your promises: Never disappoint those who work under you.

- Lead by example: Encourage cooperation, giving back and love in your team. Don't forget to lead by example!

A leader is someone who can direct human efforts in the best possible direction to achieve the best possible outcome. A leader looks at the pros and cons of a situation as well as the different ways of accomplishing goals, and should effectively communicate these to the team. Therefore, strong analytical skills and a process that the team can understand well are important. As a leader, I never ask anyone to do anything I would not do myself. If I ask for something to be done—I am 100 per cent responsible if something goes wrong, having directed this action.

It's also important to compensate everyone involved fairly, and reward them by telling the team or person what they did right along with monetary compensation.

Finally, stay on the project until it is done, because as a leader, there might be challenges that need answers that only you can provide!

Above all, when you select people to work for you, trust them!

When I think of leadership in my own life, my thoughts go back to my earlier experiences of leadership in Mumbai at the St. Anne's High School at Fort, and at The Cathedral and John Connon School. At both schools, I was elected the head girl of the student council and then, at the University of Delhi, I was elected the Vice President *and* President of JMC (Jesus and Mary College).

I always thought of leadership as a service. For me, it was a way to use my skills and my 'ins' with the college administration to solve problems for other people who are of my age, or to put forward ideas they might be passionate about. Being a leader was a joy as I loved interacting with all kinds of people, understanding their different points of view and finding solutions to their problems.

I would sit in the JMC canteen, eating my chana bhatura and drinking karak chai, listening to things that were going on in college, or in other colleges and in the lives of others. If someone needed something done, they knew I was just an ear away and always happy to help optimize a situation, if it fell within my value system.

I held up certain values of honesty, integrity and rightful living, which basically meant not hurting another human, and no one could sway me from my principles. This quality of keeping true to one's inner compass that I developed at JMC in Delhi and imbibed from the nuns has literally taken me through life, keeping me 'on course' during many challenging moments!

3 TIPS ON HOW TO RECHARGE YOUR HOME AND WORKSPACE

- Put the focus on joy: Look around your room, look at the thing, the object or the piece of art that makes you happy and joyful, and move it into a central position in your room.

- Allow for spontaneity: Our energies are always changing, and we should feel free to move little things in and out of our work and our home spaces.

- Let it reflect *you*: Take a moment to make sure that your space is resonating with your current energy at that particular point in time.

It is an underappreciated fact that spaces have a profound effect on us. Whether it is our mood, our psyche or our drive—the aura of the space we are in has the potential to help us or hinder us. Our space can make our tasks feel inspired or make them feel like a chore.

Luckily, small changes can have a big impact on how our surroundings affect us. We don't need to reinvent the wheel every time we struggle to adjust to the aura of our home or workspace—a few thoughtful flourishes are enough to bring the space closer to how we want it to be at any given time.

Early in 2021, I was transitioning from my Manhattan townhouse to my home in the country, Ledgewood. While packing, I found that over twenty-five years of living in the same townhouse had produced a collection of too many paintings, objets d'art, furniture, clothes, crockery and silverware! Instead of it being a liberating experience, my impending move was becoming an overdrawn battle of dealing with things that had lost their relevance to me years ago.

On the advice of an interior designer friend, Gilbert Holmes, I took up the mantra: 'Declutter, Declutter, Declutter.'

So, a tonne of things were sent to several charities for redistribution among those who needed them the most. Perfect! What a great sense of joy and relief!

Decluttering is freeing as we let go of what no longer serves our needs in our current stage of life!

We need to surround ourselves only with things that serve our current energy. Furthermore, don't underestimate the importance of having some emptiness. Thoughts need some empty walls and spaces so the good ideas can incubate and take flight. Get rid of things! Let others enjoy them; it's okay. Just do what keeps you happily charged and motivated to get your work done!

It's also important to not forget the unseen dimension of the *aura*. The thing I do most often is that I light a scented candle, in every room each day. I use my own Giving Candle, and it changes the energy—after all, it has herbs and flowers of my choosing, which I prepared while I meditated on the aroma—and is an extraordinarily transformative tool to have in the house.

I also add a little spray of the Giving fragrance on the crown chakra and in front of the yoga mat before yoga practice or my daily meditation. The three key herbs chamomile, rosemary and basil are excellent for cleansing and purifying!

Let's give the best to ourselves and our spaces as we live fully each day of our lives!

3 TIPS ON OWNERSHIP

- Ownership is a myth: While we are on this planet, we have to understand that we never really own anything, not even real estate. When we pass away, we leave it all behind.

- Ownership is transient: We have to understand that our belongings are loaned to us by the universe to enhance our lives, and so, we should cherish the things we have.

- Welcome joy, not stress: We should not be attached to things. We should enjoy our belongings as their purpose is to bring joy into our lives and not stress.

Let's examine our relationship to material things. We own things because they connect us to people, to places, to life experiences. They provide shelter, safety and enable us to take care of ourselves and accomplish whatever goals we set out to accomplish. These things are useful while we are alive, but we must always remember that the minute we die, they are of no use to us whatsoever. The ownership of things gives us a sense of status and safety. This, in turn, help us attain our goals and wishes. Ownership, thus, has a powerful effect on the earth and the people around us as it enables us to fulfil our mission on this planet.

It is best to consider the things we own as loans. So, we must take care of these things and make sure that they are actually serving our needs on this journey of life. Non-attachment or aparigraha (a Sanskrit word for non-possession and non-greed) is an important quality to cultivate in our lives. We must remember this while acquiring ownership of homes, cars, clothes, jewellery, books, digital equipment and other worldly objects.

The biggest mistake we make when we acquire all that we strive for with hard work is that we forget to enjoy it! Don't make that mistake. Enjoy your things; you deserve it. Enjoy it without attachment, without greed, and without boastfulness or ungratefulness!

You deserve to own some of the earth's wealth. Work hard and enjoy it!

3 TIPS TO BUILD A SUCCESSFUL ENTREPRENEUR BUSINESS

- Identify your passion: Identify what you are passionate about!

- Be astute: Know when to enter and when to exit the market.

- Don't hurt others: Make sure you don't hurt anybody in the process of reaching your goals.

Success can mean different things to different people. To some, it may encompass financial accomplishments or business triumphs. To others, it may mean an unburdened heart and the knowledge of a positive impact delivered by one's actions.

The most fortunate of us figure out how to succeed at both!

I was speaking to the Greek tycoon Makis who has built a very successful global business of clothing and dyeing and has a significant presence in India as well. The Garibaldis of Florence held a dinner for me in Capri, where Makis and his beautiful wife were seated next to me. I asked him about how he started his business, and during the course of that dinner, he gave me a masterclass in entrepreneurship, which has helped me immensely in my own pursuits.

Makis told me that the way to build a successful entrepreneurship business is to first be clear about what you want to build. Then, be prepared to work day and night to accomplish your goals. Third, make sure you trust your core people. If they disappoint you by repeating their mistakes despite your timely interventions and requests, replace them immediately!

Finally, never hurt people in the process of achieving your goals.

The most important thing that he shared that evening in Capri was that I should know when to enter a business and when to exit it. Always have an exit plan at the back of your mind. Never be too arrogant to think that you will be needed forever. Things change, tastes change, technologies change, and we have to keep all this in mind. The one thing that should not change is your passion for your idea. You must bring that to work every single day!

3 TIPS ON HOW TO RESOLVE CONFLICTS

- Pause and think: Don't react. Pause, take a deep breath and think before you act or speak.

- Let go to gain: The more we let go, the more we may gain.

- We are all connected: We need to always remind ourselves that we are connected to everything else. When we remember this, conflict tends to dissolve automatically.

We live in a fast-paced and interconnected world where conflicts are bound to occur. One evening, I went for dinner with a colleague. We had been working on a joint project all day, after which we decided to go have dinner at a new restaurant that had opened nearby to treat ourselves. We went back to our respective hotels, freshened up and met at 7 p.m. for dinner.

During the course of the project, I had been independently working on a book that was finally taking an interesting shape and I felt it would be of good value to readers. I was considering translating it into a couple of languages and so had many thoughts swirling in my head, all unrelated to the project that I had been working on all day with my friend.

We were seated at Maxim's restaurant owned by Elin Nordegren, the amazing ex-wife of Tiger Woods. The restaurant was filled with the buzz of interesting people.

I started talking excitedly about my book, but it seemed like my friend was not into speaking about it. I changed the topic. After an hour, the book forced itself back into my mind and I started talking about how I would be going to India on a health trip, meet the publisher there, and even explore the possibility of translating it into several languages including Hindi, Marathi, Tamil, Telugu, French, German, Chinese and Russian.

I asked him, 'What would be a better city in Russia for the launch—Petersburg or Moscow? That is, if we do end up getting the book translated.'

My friend, who is from Russia, suddenly grew very silent and seemed upset. Upon asking him what the matter was, I realized that he had misunderstood me. He thought that I was asking if it was even *worth* launching in either of those two cities! He, naturally, felt upset and undermined. All the while, that was the furthest thing from my mind!

So, here was a conflict. First, I had to take a huge breath and pause to fully understand what he was mad about. The answer was clear: he had misunderstood; I was truly excited about the possibility of selling my book in Russia while he thought I was dismissing Russia. My actual excitement had not been clearly communicated!

I had to let go and take time to explain that I really wanted to publish the book in several languages as I had friends all around the world. As soon as I did that, my friend was swimming with ideas about how to promote the book on Russian Instagram, especially as he has many Instagram friends who are both stars and influencers. So, the moment I let go of his outburst, I gained more ground with my friend who then shared some really useful inputs with me.From this experience I learned that when working on interconnected projects with people, conflict has to be resolved quickly to move on to other projects that are in progress. Letting go of another's outburst is a really sensible, mature thing to do.I think I do have an affinity for problem-solving. I learnt to do this at The Cathedral and John Connon School in the twelfth standard. We had all been studying rigorously for the upcoming board exams, so my classmate, Vivek Vaswani, suggested that we bunk the last two classes and go out as a group to see a movie. I was a bit scared, especially as I was the head girl of the school, but I was soon convinced. Other friends were going and the movie was only an hour and a half long, after which we would come back to oversee the house games for the juniors and all would be fine!

First note to self: if your intuition says there might be trouble, do take a moment to listen to it. That day, I did not listen to my intuition and about a dozen of us went for a movie. Shalini D'Souza, Sheila Juwadkar, Vikram Gandhi, Phiroz Dubash, Vispi Patel, Nitin Jasani, Somi Hazare and Deven Khote, Anurag and Tarang Jain, and myself.

The movie was funny until suddenly one guy who had been sitting one row ahead of us said that that we had put our feet on the seat in front of us, and that our shoes had been touching his seat for the entire duration of the film. His brother stood up and said they were offended and that they had to take back their honour.

In a flash, he ripped Phiroz's shirt while the other moviegoers shouted at us to shut up.

The manager arrived and asked us what the problem was. Somi immediately took charge. He told the manager that these were his rugby friends whom he had not seen in a long time. Somi gestured to us to keep filing out of the theatre.

Outside, Somi thwarted every effort by the goons to harm us. 'Hey,' he said to the gundas. 'What are you doing tomorrow, after school? 4 p.m?'

They said nothing.

'We'll meet you in front of the wall outside our front gate. We will have a surprise for you.'

By this time, I was wondering if there was more drama unravelling on the screen in the theatre, or before me in real life!

'We will be there,' they said. 'We are not afraid of you stupid, private school types and we'll take your girls too.'

Somi, smiling throughout, said, 'Okay, till tomorrow!' and we ran, cramming into two taxis and rushed back through the Bombay Gym squash courts side entrance so we could sneak back into school.

We were fortunate that no teachers were upset. However, the difficult situation was handled by Somi. He came up to each of us and collected one rupee, fifty paise, ten rupees and so on, and then he asked the snack guy at the gate to roast his best peanuts and chana with onion and lemon and cut the best raw mango, 'kairi', complete with salt and chilli.

When the guys arrived, ready to fight, Somi had these snacks ready and soon they were eating them and drinking chai! Rumour has it, they invited Somi to play in their Marine Lines kabaddi team!

So, we truly have thousands of ways of resolving conflicts!

3 TIPS ON HOW TO KEEP GOALS REALISTIC

- Evaluate your goals: A goal *must* excite you, *not* overwhelm you.

- Keep your goals exciting: The drive to accomplish a goal should motivate you.Nurture goals: Remember that goals are important for survival and a healthy self-esteem. So, nurture your goals carefully and stay focused.

G oals are a simple way of organizing our desires, ambitions and aims in life. It is easy to be swept away in the whirlwind of life and lose track of what we want to build towards. We make goals to remind ourselves to stay true to the decisions we take in our psyche.In January 2018, I decided that I needed to set a multitude of goals for myself. Each goal I set would have taken a year each to complete, but I decided that I would work on all of them simultaneously. After all, each goal was connected to the other in some way. Each goal was intensive: the first was developing branding and packaging for a new mission-based fragrance line I wanted to launch, the second was renovating my home in Manhattan, the third was renovating another home in the country, the fourth was spending time with my grown kids who by then had their own apartments across different cities in the US, the fifth was responding to a television show sizzle that some producers had approached me for, and lastly, maintaining a healthy weight and planning to get enough sleep every night. To these, I also added another goal. I wanted to explore another partnership for the Giving Back Foundation in upstate New York.

I was very happy when I wrote down my goals, but as I went through the year and started achieving some of them, I realized that I was putting less time into my health, sleep and exercise. I had listed my goals, but I had not prioritized them well enough. I began to feel tired, even though I was quite excited that I was making good progress with the things I had set out to do earlier in the year.

So, I went back to my list and started reorganizing those goals. Prioritizing them better. Putting family, health and wellness first.

The year was super smooth after that! The excitement of the journey was back and I was no longer focused on the destination. The key is to do our best every moment, and the outcome will automatically be good.

I felt good. I knew that my goals and life were back on track!

3 TIPS ON HOW TO BE ASSERTIVE WITHOUT BEING UNKIND TO OTHERS

- Be firm but kind: Be clear about what you want, but also be mindful of others.

- Have clear intentions: Know within yourself what you need to do and think of ways of doing it without hurting anyone.

- Set personal boundaries: Personal boundaries are silent but strong assertions in themselves.

We are all on a personal journey towards fulfilment. Thus, it is inevitable that our desires brush against the desires of someone else, and so, create conflict. We must remember that such conflicts provide us with an occasion to empathize with our fellow traveller, and not see this as an opportunity to engage in anger or any negative emotion. We can still get what we want, and we don't have to hurt or put anyone down to get it.

Boundaries are something I find very hard to execute and live by in my own life. By nature, I am a kind person who can be firm, but too often I am swayed to help others beyond my real personal capacity. This has caused me a lot of stress, as it has often been hard for me to say 'no' when people have reached out with their problems.

Other people's expectations make saying 'no' a little harder for me. Being CEO of the Giving Back Foundation, I have experienced some non-thinking people say things like "You are a giving back person, how can you say no to me?", or "Why are you telling me that I am late for an appointment?", or "What, can't you help me?".I have to calmly explain to myself and then to others that I don't often have the bandwidth to help. Sometimes it is as simple as starting a meeting on time to help complete the meeting in the given time. The latecomers have been annoyed by this but over the years I have realized that the best way forward is to stay on the path of truth. It is the correct path.

I have set certain personal boundaries for myself. They are silent but firm. For example: if I have been up since 5.30 a.m., have worked a full day and am exhausted, and after dinner my friends say it's only 11 p.m., let's go to such-and-such new place, I politely decline and go home to rest, no matter how much I am pushed. I definitely feel that I made the right decision the next day!

Boundaries are not about upsetting other people; they have more to do with making the correct decisions for ourselves. Once we know and understand this, it's both a joy and an easy process, and usually, all parties gain through this process!

When I think of being assertive without being unkind to others, my thoughts go back to New Delhi in 1984. Padmini Lulla was the leading agent to scout amateur talent for print and movie ads. I had done a number of projects with her successfully, including Pan Ketchup and Hero Cycles. She called me up one day and said that she had a very lucrative modelling campaign for me, and the four people she had picked had to meet the sponsors at her office.

I got there quite excited, but I did not know the product. When I arrived, they explained that it was for a popular Indian brand of cigarettes.

I immediately said, 'I am sorry. I cannot do this ad as I believe that smoking is very harmful to our health.'

Padmini looked at me, smiled and said, 'Are you sure? This job pays ten times more than the other assignments you have done.'

'Yes, I am very sure,' I said.

'Okay, then. No worries, we will try to get another model here to meet the sponsors today. Here is your travel fee and thank you for your time.'

This is how I have set my personal boundaries, and Padmini Lulla, who being a real professional, totally respected that. So will others in her place. Padmini, as I have been told by my friends, has spoken to others about this incident and said that she has always respected me for my decision.

ON LIFE

3 TIPS TO CREATE RAINBOWS IN LIFE

- Love all beings: Love in action is like a beautiful rainbow without an end.

- Accept everything: Sound, light, breath—everything on the planet vibrates on a certain frequency. When we accept things, it only means that we are choosing to vibrate on the same frequency as the situation. This is a rainbow in formation.

- Serve from the heart: Serving from the heart creates a rainbow wherever we go!

In August 2018, I was in Jupiter, Florida, enjoying some rest, exercise, yoga and meditation. My youngest child, Kabir, had just graduated from Harvard and my daughters were happily at work—one of them in the field of music, and the other lobbying for organic farming—as they were determined to contribute to the world!

With my children settled, I felt that my primary responsibility as a mother had been met and that I needed to continue working globally and use the Giving Back Foundation better to serve more sections of humanity on various levels. But how? I felt stuck. No donations were coming into the foundation, and while my TV show was moving forward with thirteen episodes on B4U TV, it was still not quite the correct format. Also the fragrance line that I had spent millions on developing was not in the right place to hit the market.

As I was sitting outside on my patio overlooking the golf course, I noticed how everything looked fresh and green and renewed. It had been raining all night. Just then, the biggest rainbow I had ever seen appeared in front of me. It was mesmerizing. In that moment, I was totally awestruck!

Time stood still and I don't know how long I spent looking at the rainbow!

It was my instinctive Noah's ark moment when God said to me, 'Move forward in faith, my child.' I realized that I did not need donations to continue my mentoring work. COVID-19 had stoked concerns about mental health issues and the tips I had been posting on Instagram had started to resonate with a lot of people. The rainbow showed me that I was on a simple, but correct path; and that it was the best way I could help people.

Since then, rainbows have been my guiding light; the signs are everywhere when I need reassurance. Now, I want to create rainbows for everyone around me so people can grow, be happy and feel fulfilled just like I feel! It was a simple shift. So, look for your sign and let it guide you further! There are signs everywhere to guide you, as Oprah Winfrey attests in her book.

3 TIPS TO CELEBRATE LIFE

- Be aware of life: Actively think about your life and choose the moments you want to celebrate.

- Celebrate others: Make sure others are celebrated; when we choose to celebrate others, we automatically feel a sense of lightness, a sense of joy and even a sense of euphoria.

- Choose positivity: Celebration is a state of mind. Choose to be positive and choose to celebrate every moment. It's in our hands.

L ife is precious. This is said so much that often these three words lose their meaning and the sentiment is taken for granted. But we must concede that life is indeed precious, and in the vast expanse of endless space and infinite time, life is also rare. Thus, we should take time out of the pursuit of routine life to remember to celebrate this beautiful gift of life by looking at nature and treasuring each and every moment.

For my twentieth birthday, I expressed to my father that I wanted a family picnic on Badkhal Lake in Delhi. I thought it would be a small group—my brother, sister and my parents—picnicking by the lake. January in Delhi is usually very pleasant. The weather is perfect, the worst of the winter has passed and the season dips its first toes into spring. As the days rolled up to 28 January, my birthday, there was some secrecy in the house. I had not been involved in all the planning. The day of my birthday arrived and there was a huge bus outside our house. My bedroom in Moti Bagh faced the main road, so I was the first to see the bus pull up.

'Strange,' I thought. DTC buses usually stay on the main road.

Then, my parents came out and when we got into the bus, Usha baji, one of my favourite aunts, wished me 'Happy Birthday!' in a shrill voice, brimming with excitement. 'We are all going on a family picnic to Badhkal Lake.'

Surrounded by my family and extended family, my parents had created this extraordinary celebration for me. Complete with our helpers, the gas range and the fresh food cooked on site, it was a marvellous day of celebration that stands out as a particularly memorable day in my childhood. We swam in the lake, ate and chatted merrily and then, exhausted, we started to head back around six o'clock in the evening. We arrived home at 8.30 p.m., and soon, I tumbled into bed—exhausted, happy and full of gratitude to my dear parents who always went the extra mile to make our birthdays so very special! Here's to life and celebration!

3 TIPS TO STAY ACTIVE

- Do something physical: We all know how busy our lives can get. We're commuting, working long hours, getting up early, getting home late. However, it's very important to be active. So, just go out and do something physically invigorating, no matter what time it is, morning or night.

- Do what you love: Do something that you love. Dance to music, go on a bike ride, practise martial arts, or do yoga. Just do something that you love doing.

- Work as a team: Do something with a team. Studies have shown that activities that are done in a team have a long-lasting impact on our mind and we tend to keep up too. What is good for the brain is good for the soul!

Health is one of the most important gifts a person can enjoy on earth. It is almost a passport to happiness. And while our bodies are resilient testaments to the universe's passion, our health can often be fragile. Taking care of ourselves is, indeed, our duty towards the divine.

When I was growing up in Mumbai as a teenager, one of my closest friends was Seema Poddar Agarwal. We used to bike to the Colaba sea pool in Navy Nagar. After biking, we would swim, have a

Rodger soda and bike back. On the way, we would talk about things, mostly nature, as we both loved watching birds, looking at the ocean waves for hours and observing the Bombay crabs in the sand. This had a profound effect on my psyche. I understood that when we exercise and move ourselves to do things that bring us closer to nature, we are joyful!

Today, when I speak to groups of young people, I find myself telling them to do things as a team, to find joy in movement, and it all goes back to those many happy hours of biking in my youth in Mumbai!

Staying active by doing something we love reminds me of the year 1998. I fondly remember my family life in Mumbai in 1998 when being active meant taking a very unusual step! Kabir, my youngest child, was a year old and I was looking for a preschool for him. We looked at West Wind but it was full, and another prospect, a woman starting a new preschool in Mumbai, had to return to New Zealand. With the days passing and no preschool for Kabir, I decided to start one myself. I wrote to a preschool in New York City to request a curriculum and started hiring teachers in Mumbai. I put the word out and had twenty students right away; and then I had to close the roster. I had a fantastic baby nurse, Sister Pramilla, who kept medical records for all the children (mostly from overseas and so it was really useful), and a local doctor, Dr Balsekar, who would come in to meet the international mothers so they knew him and where his clinic was in case of any emergencies.

With a fantastic curriculum and inspired teachers, I started the International Playschool of Mumbai and it was a very rewarding experience for me, the teachers, the students and the parents as well.

There is a funny moment from this period which I absolutely must share with you. The children were picked up at 11.30 a.m. from the preschool every day. On Fridays, we had started noticing that the driveway was crammed with cars from about 10.30 a.m. onwards. In the beginning, I paid no attention to it, but soon it became clear that many of the nannies and drivers came earlier on Friday as they wanted to meet or get a glimpse or a photo with Vivek Vaswani from

Bollywood. Vivek was a classmate of mine from high school and he taught speech and drama every Friday at our preschool! It was quite funny, and even though we requested the cars to arrive only at 11.20 a.m., this routine remained the same over the three years I ran the preschool.

I am in touch with many of the children I taught as well as their parents. They have all gone on to become strong, intelligent members of society. I think of those three years of the International Preschool with great gratitude and pride! Needless to say, those tots kept me constantly on my toes, and I never felt more active or healthier! If there is a lesson here, let it be that there is no shortage of activities we can undertake to stay active. If you can't find the right one, start it yourself!

3 TIPS ON HOW TO RISE ABOVE A CURRENT SITUATION

- Find your way out: Even if you think you are at rock bottom, remember there is always a way out.

- There's always a solution: For every problem, there is definitely a solution. This is the yin and the yang. It is the way that the world works; it's as simple as that!

- Visualize the solution: If you can visualize a solution, you can find it.

Everyone gets stuck in a rut at times. The important thing is to know how to climb out of it.

I have dealt with several difficult situations in my life, but probably none were as difficult as the year 2016, when all should have been smooth sailing. On paper, it all seemed well. My divorce was behind me and my children were doing well. I was living in my townhouse on Park Avenue in New York City. The Giving Back Foundation's work was more meaningful than ever, and a number of magazines, newspapers and editors from around the world were reaching out and calling at the office to feature me in their editorials. It was gratifying and validating. However, my soul was not at peace. I was doing too many things and was being pulled in too many directions. I was travelling too much, attending too many events and it was all making me feel dizzy, exhausted and unclear.

One evening, I lay down to sleep, and the next morning, I did not want to get out of bed. The thought of another busy and crazy day had started to make me feel like my life was not truly focused on what should make me happy. I sat down and began to ask myself: What do I really want to do in life?

Just then, a close friend called and said he wanted me to host a Diwali party at my townhouse; Sadhguru would come too and deliver a talk there. I invited one hundred and twenty of my dear friends and that evening, I received my answer. During the talk, Sadhguru said thoughts are energy fields. Think about what makes you joyful, and then, proceed to accomplish your goal. But clarity is essential.

I started meditating, calming down, and ended up producing, scripting, and airing calming information in the form of an entire season of television—thirteen episodes with the B4U TV—addressing topics such as peace, joyfulness and happiness. That was the beginning of understanding who I truly was, and possibly what my true mission in life was about.

My takeaway was that no matter how much despair we feel, the answer to the problem is always available to us. We must seek it with patience and conviction, reminding ourselves that no matter what, things will be all right if we conduct ourselves in the correct manner. There are multiple solutions to every problem.

3 TIPS ON MAKING FRIENDS

- Smile: A friendly smile is a great door-opener.

- Offer true support: Offering true and reliable support cultivates lifelong friendships.

- Expect nothing in return: True friendships should always be unconditional and non-transactional.

Friends are the refuge we find in the course of our journey of self-discovery. They are the bastions we rest our thoughts and feelings on when we are too tired to carry the weight alone. It is easy to define the value of friends based on how long we have known each of them, but time is relative. Whether you've had a friend for a moment or a lifetime, count their presence in your life as a true blessing.

Everyone knows I love being with people of all ages, nationalities, countries and cultures. I love learning from *all* people, so I am open to listening and hearing without judgement. I think of myself like a child, capable of accepting all the innocence and purity that the moment offers. I trust my gut, so if someone feels off, I just walk away. For the most part, meeting new people at airports, planes, in lines at restaurants, at conferences, at social clubs, at university gatherings, at the grocery store—any place—is a wonderful opportunity to meet and talk to beautiful people on this planet!

Once I took a trip to Maui to visit my son, Kabir. On the United

Airlines flight back to LAX, a slim, rather purposeful woman took the seat next to me in first class. She was not inclined to talk much, but being my usual Meera self I started talking to her and realized she was a very evolved human being! Anyway, she was clear she wanted to work on her laptop and not talk too much. But, when she took a break three hours later, she initiated a conversation about siblings, unconditional love, being a teacher and guide for anyone on the planet who might need guidance.

Finally, something in me made me ask, 'Who are you?' It was both a spiritual enquiry as well as a general one.

She smiled and said humbly, 'I'm Linda Woolverton and I write for Disney.'

Linda has written screenplays for *Lion King, Beauty and the Beast, Alice Through the Looking Glass, Aida, Maleficent,* to name a few! She has influenced generations of young people on the planet! I was overjoyed to meet and speak with her!

Being open to all humans brings this sort of excitement to life. It is filled with love and the possibility of making another friend any moment!

As a final word on making friends, on a one-to-one level, I feel lucky to say that I tend to make lifetime bonds. My parents brought me up with so much love and trust. It makes it easy for me to foster long-term friendships. My friendships are unconditional and non-transactional. It makes for very simple and pure friendships that end up generating a lot of happiness over a lifetime. My close friends and I tend to spend a lot of time together.

The third tip on making friends and keeping friends is that you have to be able to support friends when they need your help. At that moment, you might not need anything back, but that's okay. Help them nonetheless. One never knows when we will need their help. It's usually the ones we have helped quietly along the way who will be waiting in the wings to help us, should the need arise. Above all, expect nothing in return for your friendship, give unconditionally, love their music and their quirks and laugh with your friends as much as you can. It all makes for a glorious life journey! Here's to your glorious life journey surrounded by friends!

3 TIPS ON CREATING A BETTER SITUATION

- Act consciously: Be conscious about every single action you take.

- Fulfil what you say you will: When you vouch to do something, make sure you deliver on that promise. Commandeer your situation: Remember that we have the ability to change our situation through our thoughts and emotions.

You are a powerful being. It's true, you are. Even though it may seem unlikely at times, you have the ability to influence or even create a situation around yourself. Look around you, understand that many of the elements that surround you are optional. Be kind, be noble, but also be happy; it will only add to the happiness of others. Fine-tune yourself, and fine-tune the circumstances around you, no matter how long it takes.

There have been times when several people have been placing their demands on me—seeking my time, energy and resources. It was particularly stressful for me when I was going through my divorce in 2013. I was simultaneously trying to make sure my three beautiful and amazing children were unaffected by the worst of it. I wanted to move back into my townhouse and recreate their childhood home, decorating their bedrooms so they could continue their transition from children to young adults smoothly. Keeping so many balls up in the air with construction, paperwork, the Giving Back Foundation, my recent life in Hong Kong, London, Mumbai, Delhi and Dubai was at times too much for me. My parents were 100 per cent by my side, and so were my children, but my confusion and sadness carried on for three years.

This is when I was introduced to Sadhguru by my close friends, Shilpa and Yakub Mathews, in 2016. I started meditating twice a day and soon, I began to calm down and approach everything with the understanding that it was all a part of the universal divine consciousness. Immediately, I could sense a mental shift, and every situation around me—big and small—began to feel better and better!

I would say my mother is the best example of how to create a better situation around oneself. Having come over to India from Ireland in 1959, when mixed-race marriages in Saharanpur and small Indian cities were still unheard of, my mother was not worried. She made the best of her surroundings with whatever little she had. When Dad sailed away to sea and she was with her in-laws in Saharanpur, where most people only spoke Hindi, Mom was not perplexed. She started learning Hindi and willingly went into the marketplace with any relative who asked her to go with them to do errands. Gradually, she began to wear a salwar kameez and other traditional clothes; she had them tailored so that they would fit better.

If she was homesick, she would go to the local British bakery in Saharanpur. Her father was a baker and a good pastry reminded her of Dublin, and her happy childhood and loving parents. Throughout her life, Mom has always created the best situations around herself instead of giving in to negative situations. Her positive way of dealing with everything gave her a sense of power and control over her own life, even though many could have said that being married at a very early age, and staying with her in-laws in a small town in another country, with no common language and miles and miles away from her homeland, could have been daunting. But not for Mom. She won hearts, left, right and centre. She went to church every Sunday, introduced Christmas to her Hindu relatives, and had the whole clan accompany her to the town for an ice cream on Sunday evenings—a tradition Mom started in her new home. My father was *so* proud of her, and here they are, happily married after sixty years!

Creating a better situation for ourselves around us is contagious. It has a long shelf life and makes everything better for all those near us!

3 TIPS ON HOW TO BE MINDFUL ABOUT OTHER PEOPLE IN OUR LIFE

- Avoid hurting others: Always make sure you are not hurting another person in your life, whether you believe he or she deserves it or not.

- Be deliberate: Be aware of your choices and then be fearless, because when we are aware and fearless, we lend a lot of confidence to the people around us.

- Mind your legacy: When we leave this planet, the only thing we leave behind are our good deeds. So, it's very important that we are mindful of other people because it is the only sentiment we leave behind when we're gone.

Life has taught me that we are all intrinsically connected. We cannot hurt another person without hurting ourselves. Recently, I have been renovating my home. I have a team helping with the construction. I am always mindful of their needs and make sure that they are safe while working. I am mindful that they eat on time and don't stress themselves on the job site. As a result, they have delivered impeccable work. Deliberate actions, along with fearless and honest leadership, inspire people to give their very best. Furthermore, being mindful of other people's needs creates a win-win situation for everyone!

I grew up in India, surrounded by buas, phuphajis, taijis and taujis, mausas and mausis, and I knew all my cousins. In short, I grew up with a huge, loving extended family who, I felt, supported and loved me very much. When Aditya Kishore Bhartiya, my avant garde phuphaji, passed away, and rather too young as he was only sixty-three years old when he died, I recall how at his funeral in Delhi people did not speak about how successful he was and how much money he had made. They talked about how mindful he was while dealing with everyone, young and old. Our legacy, in truth, is only the impact we leave on those around us. So let us be more mindful of them, and ensure that we understand their needs better.

Also, one of the people I most admire in the world is Dr Mohammad Yunus. I had the privilege of meeting him at the Times Center, New York, where he was speaking at a New York Times event. My three children were with me, and he took his time speaking to them. Cultivating the younger generation is something he believes in, just as much as I do.

I have learnt many lessons while following his journey in Bangladesh, especially through the manner in which he understands the power of every human. When he started the Grameen Foundation, which gave unsecured loans to the poorest people in Bangladesh, they used the money wisely and always repaid the loan, unlike what his critics had predicted. These were group-reinforced loans, so people within the group looked out for each other and the loans were always repaid. The businesses grew, and so did the confidence of the empowered new business owners. The upliftment of everyone is the upliftment of ourselves—as we are all connected.

It is true that when we help another person grow, we grow ourselves, even if we are not aware of it. Thus, it is supremely important to be mindful of all those around us, and recognize their needs as well as our own.

3 TIPS TO MAKE POSITIVE CHANGES IN OUR LIFE

- Make small changes: Start small, whatever that means. This applies regardless of whether we're making better choices like increasing physical activities, choosing healthier foods, or reducing stress by making time to listen to soothing music and so on.

- Build regularly: Practise regularity. With constant regularity comes progress.

- Act with sincerity: Be sincere. With sincerity, we make our resolve stick.

Change is happening all the time, whether we know it or not. The right actions and the right kind of thinking change things in a direction that will have a positive impact on our life.

The year 2013 was tough for me. I had too many things on my plate: a move back to NYC, renovations at two properties, children in London, LA and Rhode Island, difficult divorce proceedings and a Foundation that was active in many countries and several live projects at once. I had a fragrance line that was now being packaged and I did not know how to deal with everything all at once. Feeling rather overwhelmed, I stopped to pause one day and decided that I would change my thinking and do one thing at a time. I would not allow thoughts of other projects and things to cloud that moment. It worked! Soon I was doing one thing at a time; and with clarity of purpose and renewed focus, I made great strides in all areas!

When I think of positive and dynamic change, my thoughts bring back memories of my mother, Ellen Mary. Mom is a force of nature! We moved to Pune, India, in 1969; and found a residence within the Institute of Armament Technology campus, which was right across the National Defence Academy (NDA). It's important for me to name these two establishments as my story involves both places.

My mother is a devout Catholic. She always took all three of her children to church every Sunday. My father is a Hindu, but he has always supported Mom's decision to raise us Catholic and said to us, 'Good values are essential, it does not matter which religious base they are taught from!'

There was no church on the campus, and the cathedral in Pune was nearly two hours away. Someone told my mother that there was a Catholic mass that was held every Sunday at 5 p.m., in a small church across the Khadakwasla Lake near NDA. My mother rode a Vespa scooter in those days; a very stylish Italian scarf fluttered around her head and shoulders.

'We will have to get to mass, so let's try,' she told the three of us. 'We will have to get there on my Vespa scooter.'

Mom held Sunita, who was three years old back then and was standing in the front. My brother and I sat in the back, holding on tightly. Crossing the lake over a narrow bridge was bad enough, but when we got to the village across the river, to our great dismay, the church sat on top of a steep hill.

'Hold on!' Mom said. 'Let's say a Hail Mary and get to the top!'

She geared up and, sure enough, got us to the top of the hill. She did this for three years and in all kinds of weather. Not once did we doubt that Mom would not be able to get us there, and then back, in one piece. She was driven by the conviction of her faith and knew that it was the right thing to do. I would get to mass and listen to the Lord's word each Sunday and we are so much stronger for that.

In these ways, we learnt that any situation can be overcome. There was always a solution and there was nothing to be afraid of.

Doing things to make positive changes in our lives is essential, and Mom gave the earliest example of this when I was just seven years old. This memory brings a huge smile to my face even now; my brother and sister just love talking about this adventure which we enjoyed together every single Sunday!

3 TIPS TO DEAL WITH DIFFICULT SITUATIONS IN LIFE

- Respond positively: Sometimes, life doesn't present us with the best situations, but we have the freedom to choose a positive response. This is what makes us a winner.

- Be selfless: The path to peace and happiness should always be above having the upper hand.

- Treasure freedom and joy: The choice of personal freedom and happiness must be above any other choice we make in life.

I had a close friend visiting my family home in Dubai. I was excited to invite my friend into my life and share the beautiful relationship I have with my parents and my siblings. At dinner on the second night, while I was trying to weave my friend into our family conversations, I noticed that he was only interested in talking to my brother's partner about their country and was oblivious to all our efforts to include him. Instead of relaxing and letting people enjoy themselves the way they wanted, I felt upset and undermined. The next day again, a similar situation transpired. I felt a strong sense of indignation and a simple matter soon became so ridiculously important in my head. Instead of meditating and letting it all go, I decided it was best to end the friendship at this point. So, I did, even though it made me both sad and miserable.

I headed back to New York, to my country home, where looking at the river and nature, I realized that I had let other people's behaviour, inappropriate as it was, affect me even though I had not done anything wrong. I was taking on their poor karmic behaviour upon myself. The minute I decided not to judge them and to be free of the negative thoughts, suddenly the situation did not seem difficult or even that important any more. A feeling of peace washed over me and I learnt that the feeling of peace was more important than the feeling of being undermined! I just needed to consciously choose!

The key to dealing with difficult situations is to step back and understand what is difficult—step away and understand the real reason for worry. And solutions indeed appear.It is the simple nature of life. Every problem has a solution. We simply have to look for it, stay centred and non-judgemental.

Today, this person remains one of my best friends and advisers in business.

3 TIPS ON HOW TO DEAL WITH PROBLEMS IN OUR LIFE

- Face it directly: Don't run away from a problem; that just makes it worse.

- Assess the problem: Analyse the issue without letting it make you anxious.

- Keep the mind calm: A calm mind will move in the direction of a solution.

There are all kinds of problems in life. Some more serious, some less so. The fact of the matter is that if it disturbs our life on any level, then it is a problem.

I have ups and downs when I regard my weight. Sometimes, during my weight swings, I end up gaining thirty pounds, which causes me great distress. The distress makes me think negative thoughts, such as, how did I stray so far and gain so much weight, was I not thinking straight? I have to learn to always be present. How am I making these poor lifestyle choices?

So the thoughts go round and round, all in a downward spiral.

Then I calm down and deal with the problem the way I deal with all problems in my life. I break it down. How serious is it? What do I need to do to fix it, and how long will it take?

Already the problem starts to feel less weighty. Hate to use a pun, but it fitted so well here. Can you blame me?

Moving along, in the case of my weight I think—okay, to fix it, I need to focus. I need to eat right, make plenty of time for fresh air, exercise and sleep early. Worry makes me gain weight. So sometimes I just need to take a break. I plan, work hard, clear out my calendar, and find a place where I can go on a retreat. Then, I just go there and focus on meditation and exercise, eating light, or just juicing for ten to fifteen days.

While cleansing my body, I make active efforts to cleanse and purify my thoughts, and make additional plans to change and simplify my life and sustain a sensible eating plan until I reach my desired weight. Yoga, walking and meditation are my route, and they work well for me—helping me to be in shape and reach the right space of mind.

One such quest brought me to Amansala in Tulum, Mexico, for three weeks. The time I spent there, living in a beach shack, has been my happiest time on this planet. I came to lose weight, which was happening anyway, but the opportunity to look at the waves, from morning to night, and to feel the water and hear the sounds continually quickly brought my body and mind back into balance with the universe.

The sunsets in Tulum are as stunning as the sunrises; the stars at night are endless! In the process of wanting to fix my weight, my journey led me to a spiritual haven first discovered by the Mayans about eight hundred years ago—where in the Roc Bay they set up a civilization that enjoyed beautiful weather, and had a bay that was safe for trade and safe from storms. The good weather, it is said, is due to frequent rain showers.

It was a tonic for the mind and the body. While dealing with one problem—my weight—I have dealt with so many interconnected problems. Taking on less, learning how to say no to some things, maintaining distance from people who don't serve a higher purpose in life, and lastly, being true to ourselves are the cornerstones to follow. Staying true to ourselves usually takes care of many of our problems!

3 TIPS ON RAISING EMOTIONALLY HEALTHY CHILDREN

- Believe in them: Believe in your children. Embrace their goals and needs, big or small.

- Trust your children: The trust of a parent goes a long way towards creating emotionally strong adults.

- Express your love: Love your children. Show them in every action that you love them! Hug them as often as you can!

Before I had my own children, I did not have any notion of how I wanted to raise children or what I planned to do to raise them well. But the minute each of my children were born, it was an instinctive and emotional bond. I understood how to emotionally connect with my children above all else. I woke every child up for school with love, fed them breakfast, took them to school and picked up after them. I listened to their daily affairs and was excited for their projects and pop-quizzes. I attended all sports events and after-school activities. I enjoyed being with my children. Being involved unconditionally has helped me nurture my children into strong adults.

Once, Kiran brought home her project. It was not graded and I excitedly asked her: 'So, what did *we* get?'

Kiran laughed and said, 'You mean, what did I get? It's my project!'
'Yes, same thing,' I remarked, smiling.
Kiran rolled over laughing. 'I got an A, Mom! Love you *so* much!'

3 TIPS TO CREATE A BALANCED LIFE

- Tune your thoughts: Take time to pray, meditate or sit in thoughtful silence for at least ten minutes every day. I meditate twice a day for twenty-one minutes and it has transformed my thinking and my life.

- Observe silence: Thoughts are energy waves! Yes, we can direct our thoughts in a manner that works for us, not against us!

- Practise moderation: Eat in moderation, sleep in moderation and speak in moderation.

In 2010 and 2011, two of the most unbalanced years of my entire life just before my divorce, I was on planes every week. Between the travel and the jet lag, I had almost begun to forget my sense of self. My daughter Kanika was in Wales, Kiran was at college in Georgetown, Washington, DC, and Kabir was at Harrow School in London. I used to be an intimate part of my children's lives while they were growing up. So, when we moved to Hong Kong, having my children spread out all over the world was a very discombobulating experience for me. I felt an inner imbalance. I was worried about Kiran in college and sad that we were not in NYC for her to come home and visit while she settled into college life. Kanika seemed to love it in Wales, but she was young and impressionable and I wanted to be sure she understood that I was always there for her. I was terrified that Kabir had to attend a boys' boarding school at the tender age of thirteen, and until that point, Kabir was quite underexposed to the world.

So, I was on long-haul sixteen-hour flights from Hong Kong to DC, and Hong Kong to London every month to be present for the Harrow exeats. I tried my best to create the environment of a loving home, and I succeeded in doing that in our London home, which I am grateful we bought since Kabir was to spend five years in London. The travel, the stress of jet lag and the lack of support from my then husband began to make me feel unbalanced to an even greater extent.

One Saturday, when Kabir had started his third year at Harrow, I was watching a soccer game at the Harrow fields. The kids were cheering each other, the English grass never looked greener and the house parents now seemed almost like family. I took a deep breath of gratitude as I saw how strong, healthy and happy my son was. I had just returned from Wales after a weekend with Kanika, and it seemed like Kiran had found her happiness in after-class drumming sessions at the 18th Street Lounge Club in DC. For some reason that moment changed me, and since then I have not allowed anything or anyone to unbalance me. I simply move away from a situation now if it's not serving my higher needs. Moderation entered my life and I have never looked back!

3 TIPS TO CREATE
ABUNDANCE IN YOUR LIFE

- Think about abundance: Know that there is enough on the planet for everyone. In other words, think abundance!

- Foster clarity of purpose: Focus on what you really need from life, then proceed with clarity of purpose.

- Attract abundance: Being *determined*, *happy* and *fearless* will invite all kinds of abundance into your life.

Abundance is more like a mindset—rather than a state of being. It is the feeling of confidence in the generosity of the universe, and the knowledge that what you already have is plenty.

In 1986, when we moved to the US as newly-weds, I had no idea of how we were going to live. We were students and our parents had provided us the opportunity and the means to study in the US. But beyond our two suitcases with old textbooks (that we threw away) and some clothes, we had no idea how our life in the US would pan out.

But we were studying hard, laughing a lot and living frugally. Without any doubt in my head, I knew we would be fine. I was pregnant with our first child, Kiran, and was acing every class in business school. I would fall asleep happy and fulfilled, like I had no worries in the world. Vikram, my husband, had started to be quite inattentive, but even that did not worry me too much. I knew who I was and had a sense that the universe was abundant. And so, it turned out to be that way.

Kiran, our beautiful first child, was born and I felt abundantly blessed and joyful as my mother and I took her out to various places in Boston in between classes and breast-feeds. I soon got a job at Macy's as a buyer in the men's department. I was to buy denim for 127 stores. Vikram got a job on Wall Street with Morgan Stanley. Wall Street was on a roll, which I did not really even know then. But life provided abundance because I believed, and somewhat unbeknownst to me, Vikram was focusing on financial success for all of us with his persistent and diligent hard work.

3 TIPS ON PACING OURSELVES THROUGH LIFE

- Slow down: Slow down just a little bit, please. Breathe, enjoy what is in front of you.

- Stay present: The past does not exist, and the future can be created in the present.

- Set your own pace: Consciously set the pace for your own life—one moment at a time. After all, we can live only one life, and that is *ours*!

L et's face it. We can't always live the way we want. After all, huge chunks of our life are shaped by external forces, people or events. As sure as the earth is round, something or the other is going to get in our path and we will have to face it. However, the universe does give us some leeway sometimes—it give us the freedom to choose the pace at which we respond to external factors. Sure, a hundred things may rush at us, screaming for immediate attention, but we can, and must, say, 'No! Await your turn!' It's in our control. We must understand what we can deal with first, and then, in a systematic and calm way, we can move on to the others—one by one.

During the COVID-19 lockdowns in March 2020, I felt a moment of panic. There was so much to be done. My townhouse was on the market. Every bedroom was filled with stuff from twenty-five years of life in this house. There was no one coming in to help. The real estate broker was not showing the house as much as I wanted her to, and the pandemic was a deterrent.

At the same time, I was renovating a house in the country. It was March 2020 and at that moment my friends would not visit me. I felt alone and overwhelmed. One evening, I went for a walk with Meryl Starr, my beautiful neighbour whom I did not know too well but always felt a kindred friendship with. We walked in Central Park and took pictures of the cherry blossoms in full bloom. I came home still a bit breathless and very stressed. I called my friends, Jaswant Lalwani and Javier Plaza, and they asked me to just relax and pace myself.

'All will be fine,' they said.

I was still stressed. Next, I called my yoga teacher. She immediately had me prepare for a bell meditation. I lit some candles, dimmed the lights in my bedroom, and we started the bell and breathing meditation session together over the phone. After an hour and a half, I finally felt more centred again. I fell asleep by 9.30 p.m.

The next morning I felt clear and decisive. I packed a bag and drove up to the country. I decided that I was going to pace myself and not try to resolve all the things in my life all at once. It worked. Step by step, every day I paced myself; I handled things one thing at a time, calmly and peacefully, and it was a good lesson. Step by step—as Rome was not built in a day. The saying had never rung more true to me!

3 TIPS ON REBUILDING

- Build it better: When you rebuild, build it better and with greater awareness.

- Build with gusto: Let your passion for your project show in every act.Forgo attachment: Do not be attached to the fruits of your labour, just build it in the very best way that you can, and in the present moment!

Nothing is permanent. Instead of fearing this basic truth of the universe, we must embrace it. We have to come to terms with the fact that everything we build will soon need to be rebuilt, especially if it still serves our purpose. This is not a setback but an opportunity to build better!

I decided to sell my NYC townhouse in 2019, and so, I started renovating my home upstate. Unsure of whether this was the right thing to do, I nonetheless proceeded to renovate my upstate house to the best of my ability—with great attention to function as well as form. As I went about rebuilding my new space with great care I realized that I was not just rebuilding, but I was rebuilding better. Now, when I am in these new spaces—full of light and positive energy, and curated to fit my family life in its current state—I feel marvellous. Hence, I say, when you rebuild, rebuild with gusto!

The above is an example of material rebuilding but, of course, we need to constantly rebuild on so many levels. Physically, mentally, emotionally and materially! All of these do not occur at the same time in one's life—though at times, they might.

Think of rebuilding like the waves of the ocean. They rise high, only to break down and rise even higher. Then they become soft and calm. Through it all, they keep advancing and never stray from their mission. We have so much to learn from the waves!

After raising my three children in India, in 2021 I realized that they were grown up and it was time to let go. While letting go is hard for any parent, I realized I could continue building my fragrance brand, a project I started fifteen years ago. The idea of rebuilding has become exciting and I am passionate about it. Getting the Giving line of products into the market and sharing them meant that I had poured my heart and soul into something I had once worked hard on and now it is time to do so again! Therefore, rebuilding is the most exciting and fundamental part of life!

3 TIPS ON RECONCILIATION

- Exercise compassion: In the words of Mahatma Gandhi, 'Compassion is a muscle that gets stronger with use.'

- Practice empathy: Express love and sympathy.

- Learn to feel unified: Work towards feeling unified. It's a sure-fire path to reconciliation.

To me, reconciliation is the meeting of dawn and dusk; the differences of night and day meet in beautiful harmony and create great splendour in the process. It is natural, it is powerful, it is inevitable. Reconciliation is transformative and healing. It is absolutely necessary for the soul.

As an Aquarian, conflict is something that is very, very difficult for me. I struggle within when I have to interact with difficult people. At times, people do not deliver, do not meet set expectations or are simply lazy and unethical. I don't judge, and I have learnt to exercise love and sympathy to resolve conflicts with compassion. It has proven to be the most effective way of resolving and reconciling with people and problems.

I recall a time in the third grade in St Anne's Convent in Pune when I was eight years old. I was chosen to be part of a 'garba raas' dance for the Prize Day celebrations coming up at the end of the year.

We were a group of twelve, and each of us were given two sticks. After every eight beats, we had to turn to the opposite partner and continue the movement. Simple enough.

However, after every fourth turn, I would get confused and either turn too late or turn to the wrong partner. This happened even after a few practice runs.

The teacher stopped the music and called me over to her desk.

'Why are you making the mistake?'

'I don't know,' I answered abashedly.

'You have to remember to turn, otherwise, you are wasting our time,' she said, and with that, much to my utter shock and horror, she slapped my right cheek very hard. The slap stung me and my eyes filled with tears. 'Go back to your place and don't make a mistake this time,' she said savagely!

I mustered all the sincerity and focus an eight-year-old has at hand, and I began the dance again. When it was time to turn, the teacher walked to my spot, which quickly enabled the correct turn and soon the dance was completed without a mistake.

'Once again from the top,' she directed, and we did the dance again with no mistakes! Whew!

'Okay, we are done for today. Get your shoes and go back to class,' she said.

I got my shoes and then, as I was walking past her I gave her a smile. She was puzzled and perplexed by it, but she said nothing. I was halfway out of the door when she called me back.

'Meera, wait please. Come back. I would like to talk to you.'

Unafraid, I walked back to her, still smiling. She said, 'I was unfair to you today. Instead of explaining the step, I slapped you, yet you smiled at me. Why? Most girls would not even have made eye contact.'

I answered. 'I knew you were trying to get us all to do the dance right. I kept making the same mistake. I kept staring at a bird on the fourth turn. I got distracted and missed the step each time. You slapped me, but Jesus always says that we should turn the other cheek, not respond with hate. We just learnt that yesterday. Besides, I really do like you!'

The teacher started crying and gave me a hug.

'Who even are you?' she said. 'Would you like to come to my home and have hot lunch with my family today?'

I agreed. We then went down to the principal's office. There, we called my mother for permission. I went to her house, and to this day, I remember what I ate. It was mutton biryani on the floor—boori style—with yogurt and pickles. Hot, spicy and delicious. Her three children joined us too. I shared my sandwiches and a red apple with her kids and, as a meal, it has always stood out in my mind!

On the day of the performance, we danced really well and received lots of claps and whistles. The teacher went on to recommend me to lead most other events. The confidence I acquired from this experience has since helped me take lead roles in not only plays, but also the students' governing body.

We had built a bond over a single incident and the bond went a very long way! It continues to serve me till date.

This is my earliest recollection of reconciliation. It's pure, it's powerful, it's freeing and one never knows what joyful things follow such a wondrous moment—so it's important to always try.

3 TIPS ON OVERCOMING BIAS

- Don't pre-judge: Always be courteous and respectful, even if you have some reservations about someone.

- Look deeper: Let's remind ourselves that the cover is not the book.

- Celebrate differences: Differences add greatly to the texture of our life.

I was headed for an interview at Harvard. At a certain point in time, I wanted to move from the Boston University MBA programme to the MBA programme at Harvard. I got to the admissions office at 6.40 a.m. I was early; my interview was at 7 a.m. Dean McArthur, Dean of Harvard Business School, had even made an opening introduction on my behalf.

I was changing my shoes in the waiting area. As I was doing so, a lady walked in. As I was changing my shoes, I asked her where Room 101 was. She told me where it was, put some lights on, and then she walked away.

When I was called in for the interview, I saw that she was the interviewer!

The interview, obviously, did not go well. I had left a bad impression. I had not greeted her outside the office or said "Good morning". I was a bit self-absorbed and nervous. Therefore, I had simply asked for directions. She was clearly not happy about that.

I have never made the mistake of underestimating a person in my life again!

3 TIPS TO ENJOY YOUR DAY

- Wake up and smile: You have to actually do this!

- Embrace the weather: Come rain or shine, enjoy what the new day brings.

- Experience the day mindfully: Remember that the day will not return, so explore every minute fully.

As I get older, I understand the journey of life better. I learn to be in the moment and truly enjoy the present. In 2016, I did the Camino walk in Spain. I was on a fourteen-day walking pilgrimage or a padyatra. They were long days, spent walking thirty kilometres. When I finally reached and walked into the cathedral at Santiago, Spain, where the bones of St James are encased in a cave below the church, I realized that I did not feel the elevation that I had expected. I then spent time reflecting on the journey—the walking, the conversations, the scenery and the joy of actually having walked the entire way! I then realized that it is the journey, and every moment of the journey, that defines the destination.

Don't expect the destination to provide you with more joy or meaning than the journey you take to reach it!

I would like to share two more instances of enjoying my day. One from my youth in India and one from a day in Mexico.

In 1979, I was dating Vikram Gandhi, my high school sweetheart. He was the man I later went on to marry. I have three children with him, although we went through a divorce in 2013, thirty-four years later. In any case, I remember a day during the monsoons when I went over to Vikram's parents' apartment in Cuffe Parade, Mumbai. We had planned to go to the Naval Sea Club in Colaba, which was the swimming bay part of the Naval Officers Club that my father belonged to.

It was raining quite hard and the rain showed no signs of letting up. Vikram was disappointed that we could not go to the club in Navy Nagar; I was a little disappointed as I don't like to change plans too much. But as we both sat there and looked out of the window at the torrential rain, we became mesmerized by it. It is an understatement to say that we became one with the rain in the most platonic and simple way. Two 15-year-olds just staring at the rain! I can still vividly experience this quiet moment of stillness and happiness. We felt the sheer simple joy of watching the downpour from the apartment's living room window, of hearing the sounds of the majestic pelting, and the claps of repeated thunder; and watching the darkening of the sky. It was nature unfolding in all its mystic beauty. We sat there for hours, silently watching and admiring the beauty of the rainfall. Yes, that day still stands out in my mind. It was the sheer joy of watching nature.

I still think about that incident, sitting and experiencing nature. Even today, when it rains or snows I am spellbound, watching in sheer wonder.However, in Tulum one afternoon, I was down with diarrhoea and cramps. I was quickly sent to my room to take two tablets of Treda. I had gone there for the yoga classes at Amansala, Tulum, which I love. Now, knocked down by Montezuma's Revenge—as it is called here—I was stuck in my room. I took the two tablets and opened my curtains and realized that I was right on the beach. I realized that I was literally living in a thatched roof shack on the beach with azure views of the Caribbean Sea. This was something I had always wanted to do.

I took a deep breath. I had been here for nine days and all that time had been spent in running from one class to another, leaving me with virtually no time to stop and soak in the most stunning views and sounds of the ocean. But the ocean is so divine!

After a few days, I woke up in the morning having entirely recovered and full of joy.

My illness had forced me to relax and to take the time to soak in the energy of the blue ocean, the soothing sound, and the mild breezes that sway the palm trees outside the terrace. It was all just *so* beautiful and stunning! All I had to do was to enjoy it and just take it in. Wow! The timeout taught me a lot.

I reflected as I enjoyed my last day on the beautiful Tulum beach. If I had not fallen ill, I would have missed these sights and this experience.

ON SELF

3 TIPS TO ATTRACT POSITIVE VIBRATIONS INTO OUR LIFE

- Use your senses: It is important to see the best in everyone.

- See good in others: Speak kind words about everyone.

- Think with love: Think about every other human with love and respect. This will automatically attract positive vibrations into our lives.

String Theory has popularized the notion of all matter existing as a consequence of vibrations. We, as humans, are no different. We exist on a similar plane.

I am aware now that we all have the power to trigger vibrations to suit our needs. Take an example. My daughter was working on her music—a remix album—when she came to stay with me in New York City in early March 2020. She was very busy and had a stressed, jacked schedule with very early a.m. and p.m. zoom calls. I hardly saw her and I was also feeling stressed because of the pandemic.

One morning I went out and bought her some yellow flowers, which I kept in a vase in cold water. Then, I took the vase up to her room and quietly placed it on her work table. An hour later, she came to find me and said, 'Mom, I love you so much. Sorry it's been so hectic. Can we eat dinner together in Brooklyn?'

For those of you who don't know, I love eating in Brooklyn!

Long story short, through my positive vibrations, I attracted the outcome I wanted and Kiran, also known as Madame Gandhi, got a well-deserved break from her work schedule too!

3 TIPS TO INITIATE AND MAINTAIN A YOGA PRACTICE IN OUR LIFE

- Maintain a schedule: Put aside some time for yoga practice every day. This type of prioritization gives us time to be still and present each day. When we build this into our day, it reinforces how important our health is for us.

- Start easy: Start with a simple yoga asana and enjoy stretching your body every day. Enjoy your practice.

- Read something positive: Try to read something that is spiritually uplifting, or calming every day. This will ensure that you are united in body, mind and spirit.

The ancient practice of yoga is one of the key respites we have from modern life. And, anyone can fit it into their day. It is relatively easy to get into, supports all body types, and it respects the person that you are, while acknowledging the person you envision yourself to be. It aligns our mind and body to the present moment using our own breath.

Yoga has gotten me through the most hectic and confusing times— such as January 2021 when I had to finally move out of my townhouse in NYC.

The staging company was three days away. I needed to have the house renovated and cleaned. The paint work was particularly off schedule. When I walked in, I saw the main painter chatting on his phone. It seemed like he'd been on the phone for a very long time.

A bit stressed, I wanted to walk up to him and say something. Instead, I went upstairs, closed myself in a room, and did forty minutes of yoga. When I finally went downstairs, I was calm and I told the head of the team that I needed them to finish the renovation on time.

He smiled. 'Yes,' he said, 'I was on the phone and I have already found two more painters to come in over the weekend and we *will* get this done. I was on the phone trying to get them both here tomorrow and I have convinced them to stall their other project and start here tomorrow!'

All was well! The energy was positive and yoga had made me calm. I had allowed the power of yogic energy to prevail! Instead of letting stress get the better of me, I let the power of the universe show me the way ahead. The power of the universe almost always leads us to the right solutions. Yoga had saved me yet once again!

3 TIPS TO TRANSCEND ONESELF

- Practise goodness: The ripple effect of good actions takes us to a higher vibration. We become part of a greater whole.

- Push beyond your limitations: If we push a little bit beyond our limitations—just a little bit more than we expect—it helps us transcend our present limitations.

- We are bigger than ourselves: Knowing we are part of a greater whole gives us the liberty to be a little bit more than our self.

I was going through a period of my life where many of the decades-long projects, like my mission brand fragrance, a TVshow about meditation, and an aware life, were suddenly coming to fruition! My confidence was shaken because of the divorce and the fear of success was holding me back, but I had to work on my fear and tell myself, 'I am only the channel through which a greater mission is fulfilled in the universe. I am a tiny, tiny particle, but I must do my bit to share the ideas I have.'

Thoughts like these give me the confidence to proceed! I continue to pursue my ideas, and more often than not they have worked out very well.You too must stay the course calmly.

3 TIPS TO CULTIVATE FREEDOM IN OUR LIFE

- Make choices consciously: Be aware of your choices. When we make a choice, we determine whether that action, word or thought is going to set us free or bind us. Choose wisely.

- Let go: We simply cannot control everything. When we realize that there is a power greater than us, we allow ourselves a certain freedom to exist.

- Practise santosha: Santosha is a feeling of contentment; contentment sets us free.

The universe often chooses for us, but we also make choices and carve out a path to reach our destination. This is the freedom presented to all of us. The question is: how will we use it?

Most of my life I have felt like I needed to control things. Then COVID-19 happened, and I realized that we don't *really* control anything. However, if we stay calm and content, we will be able to make the correct choices for ourselves. This, in turn, will be good for the universe as we are all connected. This awareness has brought me a sense of freedom, a freedom I can experience while being connected to everything.

As I look back on my life, it is clear the good choices we make in the moment with our consciousness intact lead to the best outcomes. In 2011, I was in London, and my ex-husband and I were planning to attend a birthday party in Europe. The day before we were to leave, my son, who was in boarding school, fell ill with a high fever. I drove to his boarding school to pick him up and bring him home.

Despite our friends insisting that we attend the birthday party, I decided to stay home in London and take care of my son while my ex-husband went to the birthday party in Germany. I was home to tend to my son, even though there was a lot of pressure to go. This conscious choice proved to be the right one to make. My son's fever soon subsided with medicine, rest and home-cooked meals. Three days later, he was strong and ready to go back to school. Had I not stayed back, he might not have recovered so quickly.

This is such a simple anecdote, but through it we all can reflect on the many choices we have made in our life. Make self-aware choices and they will usually prove to be correct!

3 TIPS TO BUILD GOOD KARMA IN OUR LIFE

- Make choices consciously: Be aware of every choice and make the most aware choice in every moment.

- Set good life goals: Well-thought-out goals are intrinsically more achievable.

- Trust the universe: Align yourself with the universe. Truly believe that the universe has your best interests at heart.

I have a wonderful anecdote to share about my friend, Hema Deora, and myself. Early in 2000, we were asked by Shobha De to participate in a fashion show called Almari. It was held in Mumbai to shed light on breast cancer, how it affects people and what should be done immediately to start recovering.

There were fabulous models there, and pillars of Bombay society had also been invited to walk the ramp alongside models. The show was to be held in the lawns of the American Consulate in Mumbai as breast cancer was an issue very close to the Consul and his wife's hearts.

We were told to arrive at 5 p.m. for hair and make-up for a 7 p.m. show. A famous make-up artist, and his team were doing the make-up for the show. I had my make-up done at home and was there, waiting for a touch-up. I bumped into Hema Deora, wife of late Union Minister

Murli Deora, and she seemed a little upset.

'Hi, Meera. How are you?' she said.

'I am looking forward to the show,' I said. 'I'm also looking for someone to touch up my make-up here backstage.'

Hema looked at me calmly and said, 'Well, I am considering leaving. I was told the make-up team is too busy with the *professional* models!'

I was really surprised by the lack of professionalism of the make-up team, but I thought the show was going to be fun. In any case, Hema is always up for a good cause.

'The cause is worthy,' I told Hema.

She nodded. 'Yes, that's why I am still here.'

Then I asked Hema if I could do her make-up. I used silver to highlight her stunning eyes, put on some beautiful lipstick, some high cheekbone powder and a stunning bindi to match her beautiful sari.

We were laughing and chatting the whole time and suddenly, the show was to start. We were being lined up. I gave Hema a big hug and we walked the ramp. Hema and I received whistles, howls, laughter and some incredible responses!

We were joined on the lawns by our children; we had dinner and then went home.

The next day, all the newspapers ran pictures of Hema, Farzana Batliwala, Shobha De and me. But there were no pictures of the models. 'Walk for a Cause' picked the social girls and the entrepreneurs of Mumbai! It was hilarious! With our humble make-up, laughter and amateur skills, we made it to every newspaper in the country!

Hema and I laugh about this even today. Karma is so interesting. We stayed to support a really good cause and we were recognized in the press with so much love, even though no one thought we were worth being made up for the show! Yes, doing the right thing in the present moment, and for the right reasons, always produces the right results. This is known as the right karmic output!

This also reminds me of another great person I've had the pleasure to come across. There is not a single Indian in any part of the world who has not grown up with his or her special Asha Bhosle moment.

Asha Bhosle is talented, kind and has a very high emotional quotient in addition to her beautiful voice. Her son, Anand, is an equally kind and interesting person. I have met Asha Bhosle on two occasions. The first time was when she performed at Carnegie Hall to a packed audience. I had the pleasure of going on stage at the end to present her with a bouquet of flowers. Later that evening, she attended a dinner for some guests at my home in New York, and despite being there right after the performance, she spoke to all the guests.

It takes a special, strong and caring person to be able to treat others so well. Performing is exhausting, but she still powered through at the dinner. She clearly believed that despite her intense efforts to entertain the same people at the concert, it was still her duty to be as friendly as possible, even though she was tired.

And, she knew how to swing the karmic pendulum her way!

In 2018, I had the good fortune of meeting her once again at the Asha restaurant in Dubai with my parents and siblings. My brother had generously arranged for the dinner tickets as it was Asha ji's eightieth birthday celebration. My father had recently suffered a stroke and movement was difficult for him. However, since he was a huge fan of hers, I went up to Anand and asked him if Asha ji could kindly come and meet Dad. He was unable to walk, but he had brought a dozen red roses to present to her.

Before we knew it, she was at our table. She chatted with my father, who felt like he had reconnected with the songs that he grew up listening to.. She gave my mother a big hug, and when I think of that evening, it still brings joyful tears to my eyes.

The power of love and kindness is infinite. It never goes away. It always stays with you. Kindness to another person is the biggest gift you can give yourself. Remember, karma is keeping score!

3 TIPS FOR PERSONAL GROWTH

- We are growing Constantly: Even when we think we are not, remember, we are definitely growing every second of our lives. It's simply how the universe works.

- Consider the acorn: Think of yourself as an acorn; when the seed germinates, it grows into a hundred-foot-tall oak tree.

- Let your goals grow: Goals that you set for yourself should be thought of as acorn seeds. When they germinate, they will produce the results you desire.

These thoughts were generated as I sat in Ledgewood, my upstate home that formerly was the estate of John Huyler. John was in the chocolate and confectionery business. Milton Hershey worked for John, and he frequently visited him at Ledgewood before he started the Hershey's brand. I was looking out at the 450-year-old oak trees that had probably seen seven generations of people come and go. As I watched these trees, I understood the metaphor of the acorn and the oak. Each of these tall trees started out as tiny acorns. Seeing them inspired me to pursue my passion with even greater gusto and hope.

I had been working on an exquisite French fragrance line for over a decade now. Fully tweaked with wonderful packaging, this is a product I believe in with all my heart and soul. I trust it so much that I have stopped buying other candles for my home, and I use only the Giving candles. I feel that the Giving candle is a unique and high-quality product that is made with love and consciousness. The notes of rosemary, chamomile and basil, and that of jasmine, patchouli and rose, are just so perfect and *clean*!

I had recently partnered with a renowned fragrance laboratory and a noted international perfume packager. Together, we moved forward swiftly, carefully incorporating my ideas and values—things like the seven chakras that exist in each one of us, as well as the colour purple, symbolizing the high vibrational energy of both our intellect and intuition—into the packaging. Finally, the sign that guides me on my way forward—the rainbow—was also added. The rainbow represents that varied people are needed to make the world a wholesome place. There are waves drawn on the products. These depict the ups and downs of life, situations we must be ready to face. Equilibrium is what the universe is moving towards, and so must we!

This is my personal growth and story, and I am committed to taking this fragrance line further.

3 TIPS TO OWN YOUR OWN VOICE

- Uphold your values: Stand up for your value system.

- Make your own decisions: Listen to others, but make your own decisions.

- Be fearless and deliberate: Once you have made your decision, hold on to it and own it.

It is unique to each person, but we all have the ability to influence our destiny in the universe. When done in kindness, karma tips in our favour. And the tool we have at our disposal, to exercise this beautiful and potentially transformative power, is our *voice*.

In 2009, when we were living in Hong Kong, Cherie Blair, wife of former UK Prime Minister Tony Blair, visited Hong Kong for events related to The Cherie Blair Foundation for Women. I am a patron of her Foundation and consider her a dear friend. One morning, Cherie and Sue Geddes, her executive assistant, were headed to a breakfast meeting on Princess Street. The meeting was a big success and Cherie Blair's speech was well received. My introduction was on point too, I might add.

We stepped downstairs, waiting for our car service to take us to the next appointment—a presentation-cum-meeting that was scheduled to begin at 11.30 a.m.—but our car and driver were nowhere to be found. These were still the days before Uber and the other options we have today!

It was 11.25 a.m. and there was still no sign of the car service, all in spite of calls made to the booking office by Sue Geddes. Just then, we saw a taxi and Cherie put out her hand and immediately stopped the taxi.

Practical as ever, she said to me, 'Well, Meera. This will have to be it if we are to reach on time. I hate to keep anyone waiting for me.'

I love how successful people have a simple and practical way of navigating the world. To them others' needs often stand above personal safety and needs. I have learnt so much while watching them. Most of them are natural problem-solvers, and they know how to react positively to every new situation—positive or negative.

In this instance, simple though the act was, Cherie Blair used her voice to decide not to wait for the car service and to keep her appointments on schedule. She refused to keep a thousand people waiting!

3 TIPS ON FINDING HAPPINESS

- Look within: We must look within ourselves to find positive feedback. This is our confidence.

- Accept your situation: Find your personal happiness through a sense of gratitude, humility and self-acceptance.

- Be thankful: Say a short prayer every night. It seals our day and connects us with the universe.

To some, happiness is the goal. To others, it is the journey. Throughout life, I have seen that if we think too much about what people say and do, then we can never be happy. This is because we are responsible for our own happiness.

I say this very often. Life does not come with a user manual that tells you 'how' to live life or 'what to do' in situations that are unclear. However, there is a sort of 'user manual' we are all born with. This is our conscience that we have to keep sharp by constantly making sure we use it to guide us. Through it, we do the best for ourselves and for others. That is the best part of our conscience. It's connected purely to the universe, so it is a win-win situation when we make decisions in good conscience. We tend to hurt ourselves and others less, and it's the simple secret to living a truly happy life!

We are taught to make 'intellectual' decisions, which might be directed towards material success or one-upping others, but the best decisions are those we take to enhance human conditions on the planet—ours and everyone else's, or at least, of the people we are in direct contact with!

So, looking within, living with gratitude and voicing that gratitude through prayer every night is our simple path to great happiness!

3 TIPS ON LETTING GO

- Allow for changes: Know that everything changes. Life is always in a state of flux and change. This is the DNA of the universe.

- Shed old goals: From the minute we are born, we are growing and changing. It's okay to let go of things that no longer serve our higher purpose. Whether it's relationships, objects or goals.

- Let things go: Don't be afraid to let go. By letting go, you open the door to many more positive possibilities!

In March 2020, when the COVID-19 pandemic hit, it was a time of flux, rethinking and repositioning for most of us on the planet. I know I have shared this moment in an earlier chapter, but it was transformational so I am bringing back the experience here again.

During the pandemic, I had moved upstate, away from Manhattan to live in my country home to avoid the highly contagious virus just like others had done. I had initially stayed back in Manhattan, even as all my friends had left the city, and then one day, I had a panic attack while walking in Central Park.

It was indeed a severe panic attack. I could not breathe. I imagined that I was gasping for air, even though I was perfectly healthy. I called two of my close friends, and both of them stopped by my house and reassured me that I was fine. However, even as late as 8 p.m. that night, I felt uneasy. So I called my yoga teacher who immediately suggested that I dim the lights in my room and put on some tealight candles so we could do a ninety-minute bell meditation together. As I inhaled and exhaled to the sound of the bells, I found myself growing very calm and clear.

The next day, I packed some clothes and my juicer, got in my car and left for the country. As I stayed in the country, I began to love the silence of the night. There was no noise. I enjoyed the darkness of the night, the brilliant stars, the pure white of the snow, and the sound of beetles, bugs and birds in the daytime. Soon, it was clear that I needed to live up here and I decided to put my house in Manhattan up for sale, despite the real estate market taking a hit due to COVID-19. It was a simple process of letting go. I had mentally let go and there was no space in my world for a home that had succeeded in accomplishing everything a house could do.

I felt a sense of freedom and clarity. I realized that I needed to declutter a bit and let go so I could move forward with my other dreams! I was so happy with my decision.

Change is the only constant, the only truth in life. Do not fear change.

3 TIPS ON IMPROVING ATTENTION

- Attention is love: The truest expression of love is attention.

- Connect attentively: Pay attention to your loved ones, your parents, your childr

- iends. Slow down and connect attentively!

- Focus on the details: Attention to detail is truly what accomplishments are built upon!

Attention is an energy, a focused assurance that we gift to someone when we care for what they are saying or doing, and when they ask for our time.

I know that when I am fully attentive, it's the highest form of love and respect that I can offer another human being. Sometimes, when I am out for dinner with a friend and I am not fully attentive in that moment, I see the quality of conversation diminishing. We then end up having conversations that kindle neither the mind nor the spirit!

This is why I always suggest that we offer our full attention as our truest expression of love!

When I think of attention, my thoughts go to one of my earliest childhood memories of my father lingering in the garden as soon as he came back from the office. We had a great gardener who used to take care of the garden, but my father had grown up in an agricultural background and loved being in the garden. He lovingly tended to the plants and flowers every day. As I mentioned before, we moved every few years as navy brats, but my father always managed to find a garden of his own so he could tend to plants. Hedges, flowers, even cacti—any living green plant was loved by Dad.

In Pune, we came home before dark and helped my father water the roses. The roses had to be watered early in the morning or at sundown. Roses, if watered in sweltering heat, will wither as they open up to receive water and cannot take too much heat. As the roses would grow and bloom, my father used to show them to us and say with great joy, 'Look at how this pink rose has bloomed!' or 'Look at the colours the petals have taken on. Pay attention, you will see the change every day'.

I used to love the time I spent every day in the garden with my brother, sister and father, carefully looking at the roses and watering the garden. Day by day, as we watered carefully, we enjoyed seeing the roses bloom and grow. We helped fertilize the soil with tea leaves; my mother is Irish so we always had plenty of tea! We usually spent teatime with Mom before heading off to play in the playground. Then the evenings were spent with Dad in the garden with Mom usually around, but she ensured that she gave us that time to spend separately with Dad. She has a special way of sharing everything—even time—which I have come to understand and appreciate.Ha, what a detour we have taken down memory lane! But this is the powerful grasp of attention. This is how moments are made, moments that we can return to, time after time in our memories.Paying attention to something, lovingly and with due care has now become a habit. Attentiveness is consciousness and consciousness is life. This is how you live in the moment!

3 TIPS TO ATTAIN
GREATER PEACE OF MIND

- Chase happiness: Seek the things that make you feel genuinely happier and go after them! Giving, being generous, and doing kind deeds are examples of such things.

- Invest in peace: We must understand that the things that make us feel at peace are also the things that endure throughout our lives.

- Forgo external attachments: Don't be attached to things that are outside of yourself.

While doing yoga I have succeeded in imbibing two fundamental thoughts.

Aparigraha: No greed or non-attachment.

Viveka: Discernment to understand what is serving our higher purpose. It's being fully in tune with our inner conscience!

These two fundamental thoughts are key if we want to bring tremendous happiness into our lives. We should not expect too much of others and we should discern what is best for us as we strive to live our best life!

I was in Florida for my birthday in January 2021, and a friend of mine from New York decided to come down and celebrate it with me.

I had planned a quiet day on the beach as a gift to myself. Among other things scheduled for the day was a massage and a reiki chakra balancing. We were going to dance on the ocean front at 8 p.m. in the light of the first full moon. We had even heard that a group of people had plans of holding a full moon drumming event.

I had the car with me the whole day as I was running errands, but when I went to pick up my friend from his hotel, he was waiting in the parking lot with the most stunning and beautiful bouquet of roses, lilacs and hydrangeas! I was touched and very surprised.

'Happy birthday, my friend!' he said. 'I hope you enjoy these flowers. I was happy to walk to Boca and back—even though it took forty-five minutes each way—since there was no florist in this area and I wanted to gift you this gorgeous bouquet that I bought in Boca for you.' I was delighted to hear this and smiled.

I felt the gratitude, love and delight behind this great thoughtful act all at once! I truly experienced pure happiness! And it all came from a space of no expectations!

This kind deed, filled with such a beautiful sentiment and so much love, will stay in my heart and mind for a long time!

3 TIPS ON FINDING
FOOD FOR THE SOUL

- Embrace tranquillity: Peace and quiet is to the soul what food is to our body.

- Learn from nature: Picture how the wind rustles through the forest, and then, imagine how it suddenly falls silent. It's nature's way of showing us how to deliver peace to our soul.

- Discipline your impulses: Know when to be still and when not to. This discipline will take you a long way in life!

Food for the soul is provided by nature—the sky, the moon, the stars, the wind, the rain, the snow and the sun! We have to actively engage with nature and experience it so that our soul remains deeply connected to the stardust particles we are truly made of! We must do this each and every day!

Food for the soul is all around us—both within and without. It could be the pigeon that trills on the window ledge, or a heavy downpour, or watching the snowflakes, or looking at the local flora and fauna. In addition to all this, I personally love reading and rereading Swami Paramahansa Yogananda's books—*Autobiography of a Yogi* and *Man's Eternal Quest*—or Sadhguru's book, *Inner Engineering*.

On my birthday in January 2021, I danced to the drumbeats under the light of the super full moon in Florida. It was an Aquarian dream! This is yet another example of finding food for the soul.

3 TIPS ON MAINTAINING JOYFUL ENERGY

- Live a balanced life: Living a balanced life is key to maintaining joyful energy.

- Actively seek inspiration: Seek inspiration actively.

- Stop comparing: Don't compare your life to that of others.

Joy comes from within. I wake up joyful being healthy and alive! I try to consciously surround myself with good people, by which I mean people who vibrate at a higher frequency. People who vibrate at a higher frequency truly care about other people and hence they tend to be joyful, conscious and happy to be alive!

Feeling healthy in our body is key to feeling joyful! I like to eat alkaline foods as they have a harmonizing effect on my mind. Pranayama techniques and actively removing toxins from my body makes me feel joyful. When I live at the peak of my health, I am laughing and joyful as that is our natural state of being. Yoga helps as well; it creates space in our atomic cells to enable them to take in more oxygen. More oxygen allows us to thrive, and a thriving body is joyful. Getting enough sleep is vital as well.

I live my own life, and I don't compare it to anyone else's. Only I can be me! These are things I do actively to stay joyful. Here's to a joyful you!

3 TIPS ON ATTAINING APARIGRAHA OR NON-GREED

- Acquire consciously: Make conscious choices when it comes to acquisition.

- Put people over property: Don't acquire material things at the cost of others.

- Heed your instincts: Trust in your instincts. Our instincts are our best guides.

When I have too much of anything in my life, I am not happy. It takes away time from living, and I ended up spending a lot of hours managing too many material things. Less is more and we must walk our purest path—even when we are not sure. The fifteenth-century poet Rumi says, 'When you start walking in earnest, the path appears...'

In 2016, I was invited to attend my first Sadhguru weekend. I had hosted Sadhguru in my Manhattan home for two Diwalis in a row—in 2015 and 2016. It's only now in retrospect that I understand the enormity of this as even I, like most people, struggle to realize the profoundness of experiences that I am fortunate to have. I usually go along with things without too much fuss or second-guessing. However, the real impact was in 2017, when I attended his weekend Inner

Engineering training in Palisades, New Jersey, with a hundred other people. Again, thinking back, it was a very small group. Sadhguru usually has a minimum of five thousand people or more in his live sessions!

That weekend, I learnt the Shambhavi technique of meditation, which has helped me quiet my mind and soul, no matter what is going on. I was also present to hear a question addressed to Sadhguru from an Indian doctor living in Florida.

He asked, 'Sadhguru, no matter how hard I work, I am always afraid we will not have enough for our old age and our children's needs. This has me kept awake with worry every night. Why?'

Sadhguru, having heard him patiently, smiled and answered, 'If I told you that I would take care of you and your wife and your needs if you come and live and work in my ashram, would you feel less anxious?'

The doctor answered, 'Yes, but that would mean giving up my practice in America, and my home, and my cars, and my retirement fund and my lake house...'

Sadhguru stopped him and said, 'Yes, all of it...to have some simple peace of mind. Would you do it?'

The doctor paused, looked at his wife and then said, 'Yes, actually we would. This way of life is making us so anxious.'

Sadhguru heard him and kept looking without speaking. Then the doctor stopped and said, 'But our children live here and it might be too much to leave and uproot; and go and live and work in your ashram. But we will give it a serious thought.'

I kept thinking, 'Aha! Here is my first lesson on aparigraha or non-greed.'

Don't be attached to anything. Leave the fruits of your good action to the universal force. Don't desire more than you need. As one practises this, it becomes a part of our natural thought process.

This is something I have tried to incorporate into my business affairs as well, especially while I considered the prices of the Giving line of products, which were to ultimately benefit the Giving Back Foundation. I have also used these principles as guides in life.

3 TIPS ON USING WATER AS A TRANSFORMATIVE TOOL

- Use water responsibly: Do not take water for granted. Water is cleansing and essential to life. Use it responsibly so there is enough left for everyone on the planet.

- Use it consciously: Connect with the revitalizing qualities of water. Take a bath or shower with awareness. Water recharges the spirit during a bath.

- Connect with waterbodies: Try to swim in a river, take a walk by the ocean, or just look at the sea. It has a lasting and therapeutic effect on us.

Water is the most vitalizing thing on this planet. When we are born from our mother's womb, we are pure vitality! We strive to stay vital throughout our life, whether we know it or not! We try to stay clean by taking showers, by saying kind words, by thinking good thoughts, by taking dips in the ocean and by drinking lots of water. All this goes a long way in keeping us grounded and in sync with the universe. This is very important if we are to maintain a connected life on this planet! So, drink lots of water, think good thoughts, meditate, practise yoga and keep transforming yourself into the beautiful vital being you were born to be!

Here is a little story that profoundly influenced my relationship with water. During friendships and associations with people, sometimes it seems like there is nothing very extraordinary about it. Until one day, looking back, something impactful happens.

I felt this during my college years in Delhi when I was attending Jesus and Mary College in Chanakyapuri. I hung out with my friends a bit—not a whole lot as we spent a lot of time with our parents who were always there for us and would spend time with us each day. One Saturday, when I visited my friend in Vasant Vihar, our group was listening to someone play the guitar. I don't remember the name of the person, but he was about twenty-seven years old and was visiting his relatives in Delhi from the US. We were listening to him play, but he suddenly put down his guitar, tore off his T-shirt, and ran out into the courtyard.

We looked outside and saw that it had started raining heavily, almost resembling a Mumbai monsoon downpour. I looked on in astonishment. In India, such a display of emotion without prior announcement was usually considered madness.

He called out to all of us and said, 'Hey, come and dance in the rain! Isn't this water from heaven miraculous?'

'Don't waste time, it will be over soon,' he said, as though cajoling us to join him in the rain.

I got up (I did not tear off my T-shirt, however!) and walked into the rain and enjoyed getting soaked. Soon, all of us were in the courtyard, laughing and talking in the rain. When the shower stopped, it was time for me to cycle home.

It felt like a renewal, a joyful transformation in a way that's not fully describable!

I started cycling home with the realization that I have *always* loved the rain, but this experience had taught me how to truly enjoy it for myself, without hesitation, without judgement and with a deep understanding of the transformative power of water.

So, when you feel stressed, drink lots of water, take a shower or a bath, or if possible look at water or images of water. It has a truly transformational effect on our psyche! If nothing else, dance in the rain or taste the snowflakes on your tongue as they fall from the sky!

3 TIPS ON MANAGING CHAOS

- Stay calm: Even in the midst of chaos, we have a choice; and we can choose to stay calm.

- Transition yourself consciously: Transitioning from the last moment to this one is a great shift, even in itself.

- Move on: Don't get caught up in the drama of life. Move on!

Chaos is nothing but a spiral of unfocused energy. It can be powerful, but it is often pointless and draining. Although there is something to learn from everything, it's best to navigate through chaos with a strong will and determination to regain the direction we want to take.

I think I have seen and managed enough chaos for three lifetimes. At times, I was even unaware of the chaos, despite sailing through it and experiencing the stress of it eventually. The way I deal with chaos or too many things at once is that I try to separate them. I rank the tasks that have to be done first, second or third, in order of priority. Once that is done, I physically make lists. Then, I roll up my sleeves and get down to accomplishing the tasks.

A key way to avoid chaos is to not discuss a task or situation with more people than you need to. It keeps the process leaner and keeps it away from too much input, which might derail the progress. When faced with chaos, I use my own instincts to solve problems so that I can quickly establish balance and equilibrium. Above all, if I am not contributing positively to the solution, I pull myself away for a short while to reflect on it and I return to it when I can be of real value to resolving the chaos or problem. The key is that I always stay calm in the midst of chaos. It is the best tool to help us make necessary decisions to resolve the chaos!

3 TIPS ON MAINTAINING
EMOTIONAL WELL-BEING

- Savour the good things in life: Let them take up positive space in our emotional well-being.

- Think positive: Actively think good thoughts.

- Steady your emotions: We should try to not let our emotional extremes rock our universe!

Emotional stability and stable thought processes are very important if we want to build a strong emotional foundation. Our emotional well-being impacts our relationships—personal as well as interpersonal, including our relationships at work. When we are in an emotional equilibrium, our work life thrives with ideas, creativity and positive momentum. When our emotional well-being suffers, we feel stuck, which can sometimes even make simple decisions hard.

In 2015, I was in a brief relationship. It initially brought me a lot of joy, but it was soon clear that it was not serving my higher path or interests. It was emotional, and it took away a lot of energy that I could have been happily directing at other fun projects I was working on for the Giving Back Foundation. I tried to distance myself from this relationship and even tried to tell the person that it was really not the right emotional space for either of us. But somehow, it dragged on for six months until one day, I sat down with him and explained to him that we were not being our best selves; we were both struggling, emotionally, and we were not able to bring out the best in us. He agreed with me, and today we are still good friends and even meet on occasions.

As soon as this relationship ended, I felt lighter, as if I inhabited a much happier emotional space. I was in peace with myself and the universe in general. I started smiling more and my work life began to flourish, bringing into play the most interesting projects, and I felt a surge of positivity within me! Emotional well-being is paramount to a joyful life on earth!

3 TIPS ON FINDING
THE TEACHER WITHIN US

- Learn from yourself: Everything is impermanent, but our inner being stays with us constantly. We are our own best teachers.

- Learn from our mistakes: We must learn not only from our accomplishments, but also from our mistakes.

- Internalize learning: We must internalize our learning well enough so that it serves us when we need the lesson.

Each of us has a teacher within ourselves. Good things and ideas that preserve life on the planet are taken forward through evolution. Ideas that are not suitable for life on the planet are dropped and fade away with time. Information is passed from one person to another—a lot of which is digital these days. However, real human growth occurs through the individual, face-to-face learning and teaching process. This process is ideal for all humans. We must try to be true mentors to our peers or to the future generations!

My style of teaching is speaking either at events or on youth platforms. I also tend to observe and suggest things to the young interns and assistants that work for the Giving Back Foundation. It's a soft and kind style of teaching. I try to make sure I never hurt anyone's feelings while trying to show a better way of accomplishing something.

I always make it clear that being careful and attention to detail are very important. The effort pays off, and things go right in the first try. Understanding the greater good of one's actions is very important, more important than just seeing how an action benefits only one person or one entity!

3 TIPS ON MAINTAINING SERENITY

- Stay unruffled: We have to try and stay unruffled despite the circumstances life throws at us.

- Understand what you control: Accepting that there are things that we cannot change and pushing hard for the things we can change creates a serene mind.

- Embrace contemplation: Silent prayer and time for contemplation helps us attain serenity.

S erenity has inspired me since I was a little girl. I would observe the nuns at the various convent schools I attended, and I always noticed that they had a calm and serene disposition. This interested me very much as I wanted to be like that—even as a child. Soon, as I went through life, I understood that this feeling is a feeling of peace with oneself and the rest of the world. There will always be circumstances that ruffle us, just as they ruffle most others in the world. But if we can hold on to our peace, it will make sure all circumstances are under control.

I was driving on I-87 North upstate to Hyde Park when a taxi in front of me stopped suddenly, causing my car to hit it. It was clearly the taxi driver's fault, but he jumped out of his car, furious. He started yelling that his taxi cab company would be mad at him. He continued to shout at me, asking why I did not apply the brakes earlier.

I listened to him calmly and smiled. Of course, I had applied the brakes just as he did. But considering the slow speed, neither of us was hurt and our cars barely had a scratch. It could have been *much* worse. If we were driving at sixty miles an hour, both of us would be in the hospital with fatal, life-threatening injuries.

'Take a calm breath, my friend,' I said.

He noted my serene attitude and calmed down. We exchanged insurance information, shook hands and went our separate ways—both of us calm and at peace. Life throws chaos at us, but we don't need to buy into the chaos and drama. We need to always be centred so that we can be the serene, divine self we were all born as.

It's the best way to enjoy life on the planet!

3 TIPS ON USING OUR UNIQUENESS

- We are born unique: We are created unique, as though from one universal energy.

- Each spirit is distinct: No two spirits are alike. Let's utilize our uniqueness!

- We can only be ourselves: Rejoice in expressing your uniqueness; and align your actions with your values and goals.

We know we are created unique. From our DNA to our fingerprints, to our irises, to almost every facet of our being—we are unique. Isn't that one of the most wonderful gifts life has given to us? We must celebrate our uniqueness and enjoy it!

I am working on my fragrance line and I believe it is truly unique. It expresses all the fragrance notes I love, mixed with herbs and flowers. It is an exquisite scent that took me ten years to create.

Now that we are in the packaging stage, I am often told in meetings that there is a 'certain way' things have been done in the fragrance industry and I must follow that route—whether that is the amount of juice in the product to the number of products in my trademarked line or the margins and the colouring.

I stop and say that it's okay. If this route has not been taken before,

I don't mind. I want to try new and unique ways of accomplishing things with a value system that is clearly aligned with mine. My fragrance has to be unique; it has to stand for my values and my idea of perfection. It has to be uniquely a Meera Gandhi product. In my view everyone will be happy to enjoy such a product, and its many proceeds will return to the Giving Back Foundation for its many humanitarian projects around the world!

So when we aim to accomplish something extraordinary, we just have to believe in our uniqueness and trust that everything will fall into place. I am just beginning to learn this.

3 TIPS TO CULTIVATE
HAPPINESS IN OUR LIFE

- Live in the present: Be in the present moment continuously. Being in the present moment continuously (or as much as possible) focuses one's attention to what's happening right here, right now. That, in itself, offers pure, undiluted happiness.

- Practice vairagya: When we cultivate the quality of vairagya, or non-attachment, in our lives, it helps to free us from mayajaal or delusion. When we are free from this, we feel happy.

- Smile: Make time to smile and laugh. It's the easiest path to happiness.

Every time I write tips on happiness, I feel that it is important to define what the word actually means to me and what it should mean to most people. Being happy is to be in a state of homeostasis where, as beings, we are effortlessly in tandem with all the other things; happiness is the absence of friction, fear, sadness or anxiety.

Cultivating happiness, therefore, starts in the mind, in our inner core. It does not spring from external things. Once we imbibe this truth, we understand that we can cultivate our own happiness by shifting our thoughts, by actively choosing to do things that we wish to do rather than by doing things we do not wish to do. We can seek to be in the present moment; after all, the present moment is always a happy moment, especially if we know we have some sort of choice in every single moment of our lives, no matter what the situation is.

My happy moment is to look at the stars before I sleep. I actively do that and understand that we are all a part of those stars. We are bits of stardust meant to shine and thrive as a part of the cosmic whole. These positive thoughts, followed by a shower and short meditation, keep me on the path of happiness and connectedness.

3 TIPS TO CULTIVATE
JOYFULNESS IN OUR LIFE

- Give to others: Consider giving something to someone else, something you know that they really need and you are able to give. It creates a tremendous amount of joyfulness. Giving is joyful.

- Stay healthy: Try to maintain good health by eating right, sleeping early, taking a walk in nature or getting some moderate exercise.

- We are one: In order to be joyful, we have to truly understand that we are not different from others. We are united as a microcosm; we are one, undivided being. That brings tremendous joyfulness into our lives.

Joy is a feeling that produces lightness of being, a desire to laugh, an ability to be playful and the general sense that it's okay that things are always changing as that is the natural order of the universe. A joyful person can see the best in every situation, and understand that the universe is mindful of everyone's best interests, and that that is how evolution happens and the planet endures. As so it goes, from one generation of people to the next.

A few days ago, I was up in Ledgewood, my home in the countryside on the Hudson River. I was up early and was looking at the river. I opened my French doors and stepped out to breathe in the first breeze of April. Suddenly, storm clouds appeared from nowhere and it started thundering. Soon, there was a heavy downpour. I looked at the rain and without thinking, I stepped on to the deck and started dancing in the rain at seven o'clock in the morning. My fluffy pyjamas were soaking wet when I stopped dancing.

After my moment in the rain, I felt elevated and started laughing as I went into a hot shower. I kept thinking to myself: how simple joy is and how often we complicate it.

3 TIPS TO BRING LOVE AND
KEEP LOVE IN A RELATIONSHIP

- Let things pass: Forgive and forget small things, even if they have hurt you momentarily.

- Love without expectations: Love unconditionally and love without expecting anything in return.

- Take a walk in nature: Try to take a walk with a person you love. The stability of nature cements the bonds of love.

The primary reason people are hurt when they are in love is that they expect the other person to be *just* like them. Love is a powerful connector and once in love, two people begin to vibrate on a similar frequency; they even begin to think similar thoughts as they share unique life experiences together.

The problems start with expectations. Each expects the other to be able to think their thoughts and feel all their feelings. These expectations become too much, and soon the love begins to wane.

Love is something that changes our body's chemical composition. One has to enjoy the moment, and the flurry of the serotonin flowing through the body. You need not worry about tomorrow or what will happen! The beauty of love is that it works only as long as it generates the chemicals necessary for both parties. When it doesn't do so, other wonderful things can be accomplished together.

However, wanting love to remain static is not realistic and this expectation sets people up for sadness unnecessarily. I think forgiveness, walking together in nature and no expectations are the three pillars that can keep love alive!

CLOSING THOUGHTS:
THE POTENTIAL WITHIN AN ACORN

I f we really meditate on an ordinary acorn, we may see the vast potential that lies within its humble little shell. What lies encapsulated in an acorn's tan little hat and within its light brown frame are all the ingredients required to become a mighty and strong oak tree.

Oak trees have the ability to serve a multitude of purposes. They provide shade, they are the foundations of the world's finest ships and furniture, and they provide nourishment. All this comes from a small acorn. It's hard to imagine that a little seed can serve so many purposes by just looking at it. And so, who knows what accomplishments are in store for each of us as we grow, year after year.

I bring up the image of an acorn again because each goal we set for ourselves is like an acorn waiting to become an oak tree. The feeling of achievement we have when we set out to fulfil our objectives helps spread positive energy throughout the world. We feel good about ourselves and this sense of achievement helps build character and form a strong sense of accomplishment.

When this feeling is nurtured in children, they grow up to be strong leaders and they support their communities. Imagine the sheer joy in a toddler's face when she has successfully taken a step and made a parent laugh with sheer delight. Her whole face lights up because she is experiencing first-hand how her actions create a reaction. When she understands how powerful her actions can be from such an early age, when the connection between cause and effect is formed and reinforced, she will be able to see how her behaviour affects a wider circle of people, not just herself.

A feeling of accomplishment is crucial for building a healthy sense of self-esteem, and we all know how important self-esteem is for everyone! Without good self-esteem, we would not have the courage to stand up for ourselves against bullies, much less be able to advocate for those less fortunate and those suffering from societal injustices such as poverty, racism and sexism. Developing emotional well-being in ourselves, our children and even those around us is just as important as any other thing we do throughout our lives.

Do not let guilt or anxiety hold you back from your pursuits. These are human constructs, which don't really serve our highest self. They exist to get our attention. They tell us that something in our life needs tending to, which then helps us get back on track. But once we are back on track, we must leave those negative thoughts behind.

We must forge ahead, much like the train as it leaves behind the platform. Platforms put us on the train, but once we are on the right train, we need to enjoy the journey and not cling to the platform. Grounding ourselves in the present allows us to look at the sights and experience the euphoria of life.

Utilize the tips in situations where you think you need some guidance. I hope they help you achieve peace, joy and happiness.

You are well on your way! Rock on!